THE CUSTOMER'S VICTORY

The Customer's Victory

From Corporation to Co-operation

François Dupuy

Indiana University Press
Bloomington and Indianapolis

First published in North America in 1999 by
INDIANA UNIVERSITY PRESS
601 North Morton Street
Bloomington, Indiana 47404

Manufactured in Great Britain

Library of Congress Cataloging-in-Publication Data
Dupuy, François.
[Client et le bureaucrate.   English]
The customer's victory : from corporation to co-operation /
François Dupuy.
p.   cm.
Includes bibliographical references and index.
ISBN 0–253–33528–0 (alk. paper). — ISBN 0–253–21289–8 (pbk. :
alk. paper)
1. Management.   2. Bureaucracy.   3. Consumer behavior.
4. Customer relations.   5. Competition, International.   I. Title.
HD38.4.D8713   1999
658.8'12—dc21   98–31070

1 2 3 4 5   04 03 02 01 00 99

Contents

Acknowledgements

This book owes much to many. First of all to the Centre Européen d'Education Permanente (CEDEP) where I have taught for over 10 years. Participants from member companies were of great help, often without knowing it, in developing and testing the ideas presented here. The Director-General of the CEDEP, Claude Michaud, has never failed in his enthusiasm and support for sociology courses in his institution. I am deeply grateful to him.

My thanks go out as well to the Kelley School of Business at Indiana University in the United States for its kind hospitality. The Department of Executive Education under the leadership of Cam Danielson provided me with the material and the human support required by the present volume. I consider it a great honour to be associated with Indiana University and the team at Executive Education.

This book presents the results of studies conducted by such top-notch professional sociologists as Touhami Bencheikh, Hélène Bovais, Yves Cornu, Valérie Dixmier, Dominique Gatto, Roland Lussey, Yves Morieux and Luiz Rothier-Bautzer. These researchers, through their work, have ensured the future of the 'Sociology of Organizations' as a consulting tool. They can be proud of this.

I would like to mention my great debt to Dominique Thomas, who provided unfailing encouragement to write and whose sociological competency is equalled only by her selflessness, patience and devotion. Her joyful manner was as consistent as her ability to correct both content and style. My thanks also to Dan Golembeski, who translated the text from the French.

Finally, everything flows from fieldwork: from all of those who, year in and year out, answered sociologists' questions, discussed their results, and were willing to speak openly about themselves and their lives in the workplace, in short, about their reality. If now in turn we are able to help them in some way, and if this book can be a tribute to them, then their trouble has been time well spent.

Introduction

Globalization and its effect on economic systems are at the centre of debates of all kinds in this *fin de siècle*. Its consequences, as we will see, are usually discussed at the level of global economies (expansion, recession, massive unemployment), or of individual economies (an uncertain future, unemployment and the related human drama, forced displacement, the redefining of work tempos and so on). Both the impact of these phenomena on the workplace, on the 'company' in the largest sense, and our ability to control and manage that impact have not really been dealt with, no doubt because these aspects are less visible and consequently much more difficult to talk about. These are the issues which this book intends to place at the centre of debate, that is, how the emergence of a globalized, post-industrial society has affected organizations – that is to say, private, public, or para-public businesses – organizations which, as the century draws to a close, provide the goods and services which people need, an assertion which many authors are currently debating. Second, through the examination of several recent case studies, we will consider how the transformation of these organizations might best be managed so as to avoid some of the tragic or painful consequences which often result from uncontrolled experiences of change.

After 15 years of teaching executives the world over, the author believes that, beyond the distressing collective and individual phenomena which the world is experiencing such as unemployment, poverty, diminishing wages, reduced social welfare and so on, it is really in the day-to-day routine of the workplace that men and women are most dramatically confronted with the fact that today's expectations of them are very different from those of yesterday. This increased instability we hear so much about not only affects people on the labour market. It also affects people in the workplace, in their relationships with one another, in the way pressure is applied to them, as well as in the way job tasks and relationships with the company are being redefined. One might object here that from this angle I am limiting my analysis to the most advantaged part of the general population, the employed. This is indeed true, but nonetheless,

1

that segment of the population plays a very important role in the evolution of business firms, and is therefore worth looking into. All the more so since, as most writers on the subject agree, that which I call in this book 'the organization'[1] is the factor best able to explain the differences, including the reasons for success, between countries and companies.[2]

Let us set the decor!

Before going any further, it is important to lay the foundations and take a look at the context in which today's organizations exist. However brief, the discussion aims to show that the profound transformations affecting organizations, which will be presented later on, are one aspect of an even more profound revolution. It has been the author's experience that, in the midst of upheaval, many corporate leaders have a hard time making this connection. The discussion should also help us evaluate to what extent, in a world where uncertainty is king, it might be useful to have better control over the parts which are nearest to us, that is to say, the collective units in which we work.

One principal fact stands out: the emergence of post-industrial society is painful, and this pain can be observed everywhere, both in the literature and in the statistics. Here are a few examples: Edgar Morin warns that 'the times are not of hope, but of falling back and despair',[3] and 'that from now on, we must confront an historic process which destroys everything'.[4] The title, of course, but also the success of Viviane Forrester's *Economic Horror*,[5] demonstrates with emotion and desperation just how difficult and frightening this emergence really is, how it can arouse in certain countries feelings of fear or aversion. Robert Castel, in his remarkable book *The Metamorphoses of the Social Question*, speaks of 'dis-affiliation' in regard to his 'history of the present'.[6] On the American side of the Atlantic, even if those who express doubt or reservation are barely audible above the ambient optimism, Jeremy Rifkin puts forth several truths which are worth repeating here. He says, 'the numbers send shivers down the spine: at the end of the 1980s, one out of four young black men was either in prison or on probation. In Washington DC, 42 per cent of blacks between the ages of 18 and 25 are either in prison or are wanted by the police. The number one cause of death among young black males is now murder.'[7] Rifkin is by no means the only one to see in these background trends now shaking the world the reasons for society's problems. Sami Naïr has no doubt good reason to claim that 'the emergence of exclusive nationalist and religious fundamentalist movements is not simply the outcome of internal mutations within each society; it is also the result spread through the media of a much deeper set of changes: that of globalization.'[8] Finally, whenever there is opposition or attempts to resist these changes, the difficult and sometimes disgraceful result is only the preservation of a few pieces of social protection, although it is likely these only briefly hold at bay the day of reckoning.[9] To symbolize this state of affairs, Robert Reich points out that in the private sector in the United States, union membership[10] has fallen to levels below those of 1930, estimated at 13 per cent.[11]

These realities, which we have only touched on here, are not temporary. They appear to be here for the long haul, at least as far as modern sociology can see. Among the possible developments outlined by Robert Castel in the part of his book on the crises of the future, 'the first is that, starting in the 1970s, salaries will continue to depreciate'.[12] The trends which seem to be taking hold, are very serious indeed. An original way to better understand them might be to look at some of the words which figure in the titles of key works from this period: *metamorphosis, end, death, crisis*. Each one expresses the sentiment, both strong and diffuse, that a world is disappearing before our very eyes, at a speed which we cannot fully grasp because we are so involved in the process ourselves.

Confidence crisis

That this should result in a real confidence crisis in all spheres and all institutions of society is hardly surprising: 'If society has today lost confidence, it is because we have returned to a financially-based line-of-thinking and have not wanted take this into account. The capital/work relationship has been turned around – money is more productive than industry. In this context, it would be absurd to suggest that work will always be available. The rules have changed, and a new system of equitable remuneration must be invented.'[13] The confidence problem is crucial. It is a topic of current debate, and I have seen that in seminars with executives, lecturers run up against it on a daily basis. The deterioration of the relationship between individuals and institutions brings with it disintegration, especially in companies, which are often no longer able to mobilize their remaining resources.[14] A goal of this book is to show how this issue might well be handled through the sharing of knowledge. Otherwise, Michel Crozier would be wrong in vigorously affirming in *L'entreprise à l'écoute* (*The Company that Listens*)[15] that the only real wealth of a company is and always will be the human element.

So as to better understand the situation, note that, contrary to a widely accepted idea, there are really very few who question the basic observation that globalization is occurring. It is only the generalization of this observation which has taken some time, no doubt because quite naturally it first had to be observed that globalization was progressively spreading its effects, even on to those who work: the mechanism was already at work in the Great Depression of the 1930s.[16] Globalization has therefore been observed for quite some time, even before the rapid explosion in technology, even before advances in communications. This was announced by Alvin Tofler,[17] and we heard at the same time of the end of bureaucracies, of the appearance of new elite groups (financial, planetary, intellectual), holders of knowledge, the 'new key to the world', controlling realms in which the outcasts – those who are 'dis-affiliated' – have decreasing access to wealth, and constitute a threat for the well-to-do. These *nouveaux riches* would even withdraw from the world – at least from the world which is not theirs – keeping it out with barricades.[18] A visit to southern California would seem to confirm these predictions.

Thus, we claim that there is agreement on the basic observation, but disagreement on the interpretation, and especially on the consequences. Between the resignation of those executives whom businesses now readily classify according to their supposed degree of adaptability, and the overwhelming optimism of the pioneers of new industries or services, there is more than a shade of difference. But it will become apparent in this book that not only do these people not work in the same types of industry – something we already suspected – but moreover they are part of very different organizations. Traditional bureaucrats whom we will meet, those in public administration or in the most traditional sectors of production in terms of their modes of functioning, are either worried, losing hope, or are trying to protect themselves the best they can... They all know well that they will not escape a very profound upheaval, not only in the 'technical' ways in which they are protected (their status as employees, their working conditions...) but primarily in the day-to-day manner in which they work together, which is the key to the revolution of organizations which we are going to try to understand through a variety of case studies. Definitely, working is no longer what it used to be!

Co-operation: here then is the keyword for tomorrow's organizations, and thus the focal point of this book. Those who, unlike the bureaucrats in the preceding paragraph, are part of businesses which have already taken the decisive step towards networks, towards a blurring of traditional structure, towards overlapping functions and the drastic elimination of internal monopolies, are perhaps experiencing more difficult working conditions, but in any case are much more optimistic about their future. And of course, between the two extremes lies a kind of tidal basin of businesses which move from one extreme to the other, at times seeking gurus, at others seeking recipes or tips which might help their leaders in their genius to spare the organization a slow and painful revolution, or at least to help the organization understand why and how it must change, and why it should be happy about it.

The anxiety stems from that which we call 'the re-proletarianization of the former proletarians'. Edgar Morin and Sami Naïr express this very clearly:[19]

> There is…the liberal scenario itself, which postulates that the negative effects of globalization result specifically from resistance to it… And so there are those who, in the fight against unemployment, advocate an increase in 'work flexibility', which in fact leads to a widespread decrease in salaries (more closely in line with salaries in the newly industrialized countries), or even job mobility (corresponding to changes in American capitalism, which is itself increasingly deterritorialized).

On the optimistic side, there is a progressive decline of the traditional way to work (industry), and an increasingly important link to society through the 'third sector'.[20] In short, there are some who see in the unremitting disruptions cumulating in this last decade of the millennium either an inevitability with unpredictable and disastrous consequences[21] or, on the other hand, a source of new opportunity which must not be missed so as to partake fully in the upheaval.[22] It is understandable that, since they were at once decisive players and simple bystanders in this tempest, human beings waver between these two positions. This is part of the short-term nature of the structural phenomenon, and is proof enough that simply being involved in a given reality does not necessarily mean we will understand it better. We will have to bear this in mind later on as we take up the matter of managing change.[23]

Middle Age or Mad Max?

Nevertheless, if the key facts and the general framework are now disputed by only a minority, then the question has become how this revolution might best be managed. There is a great deal of debate surrounding this question, and not only in Europe. The idea that the United States or Great Britain already reached 'the other side' as early as the 1990s, is both ridiculous and might even act as a deterrent. Even though the debate surrounding these issues differs somewhat from country to country, even if the reaction of Anglo-Saxon communities or of associations to the most destructive effects of the upheaval tends to keep public debate to a minimum – Tocqueville discovered this long ago – people are still voicing their concerns. After all, downsizing and re-engineering were first challenged in the United States,[24] as was the notion of an 'anorexic corporation'.[25] The arguments are sound, not controversial. Everywhere we turn the debate over the consequences of this fundamental movement which we are all experiencing is the same: 'At best the Middle Ages, at the worst Mad Max', writes Edgar Morin.[26] The 'forms of progress which destroy work' which Rifkin lists in his book are impressive[27] because of the universality of the domains which they affect. It is not simply, nor even principally, a question of capital funds which are constantly in motion, 7 days a week, 24 hours a day, entirely outside of the control of public authority, a fact which undermines the very existence of nation-states.[28] It is a matter of concern, for example, to all food production industries of all kinds, including synthetically manufactured foods, that a new technology could potentially have the same effect on a large portion of the labour force of developing countries as did the mechanization of cotton harvesting on the condition of black Americans.[29]

The American model

More differences in this debate appear when we consider how these issues are discussed in different countries. Indeed, what is at stake here is the historic and contemporary place of countries on the global economic and political chessboard. But we also see that they differ – and this is of particular interest to us in this book – in the kinds of organizations which can be found there, as well as the relative ease or difficulty with which organizations can be induced to change. Limiting ourselves to several states or regions, let us take a brief look at America in its triumph, a somewhat arrogant America; at the persistent anxiety in France and Germany; at the surprising case of Switzerland; and at uncertainty in several Asian countries.

All is going well – even too well – for Fred Bergsten, Director of the Institute for International Economics in Washington, who, while showing some pride in the healthy performance of the American machine, points out two main sources of imbalance which are dangerous for the global economy: 'There is the gap between the healthy economy of the United States and the persistent sluggishness in Japan, where there have been no signs of improvement over the past five years, whereas in Europe, which is hardly doing any better, there is mass unemployment which forced obedience to the Maastricht treaties will only aggravate.'[30] This tells us quite a bit about the 'we are the champions' attitude displayed by the United States in the 1990s, a great cry going out as if from so many fans at the Superbowl. Many possible explanations have been offered for this victory. Two of these are of special interest here since they open pathways for understanding 'the last of the bureaucrats'. The first, naturally, we might say, is that of the increasingly precarious nature of the labour market, of salaried employment itself, and of the decrease in salary levels. In 1993 alone, out of 1.23 million jobs created in the United States, 728 000 were part-time jobs only, really little more than 'side' jobs, accepted by those who were in fact seeking full-time employment.[31] Robert Reich, for his part, notes that inequalities in revenue increased in America from 1977 to 1990, when average income before taxes of 20 per cent of the poorest Americans decreased by 5 per cent. At the same time, the income of 20 per cent of the richest Americans increased by 9 per cent.[32] Rifkin adds that between 1973 and 1993, working-class Americans lost on average 15 per cent of their purchasing power.[33] Both authors agree that one of the conditions which made these changes possible was the deep, long-term and unprecedented weakening of the union movement. The figures are neither cause for celebration nor for sorrow. It is simply a sign that today, when we see the word 'change', and when opposite this word we are presented with examples – 'the success stories' – they are best understood in terms of 'less', for they have been achieved at the cost of the renunciation of advantages, of security and of comfort. Bureaucracies, whether of the public or private sector, are characterized by the advantages which they have obtained for their members, the 'pluses', even if the customer has had to pay the price of these pluses, not only in terms of the basic cost of a given service, but also in day-to-day terms of business schedules, of the speed of delivery, of the quality of the product or service or, to make it short, in terms of convenience. We will return to this idea later on.

The result of all this is that 'opposition to change' is not an abstract, psychological problem, but in fact a rational strategy,[34] in the sense that the actors who develop such a strategy struggle to hold on to something. Even if what they are trying to hold on to comes with a price, due either to the association or the customers as mentioned earlier, one cannot naïvely explain to these actors that their future will be more fair and above all, 'better', if only because in the short run at least, this is not true. Clearly, the more that organizations come up with different kinds of benefits for their members, the more difficult and costly it is in human terms to give up these benefits. This will lead to some methods for managing change which take this into account.

The second factor which America of the 1990s considers to be crucial to its success is the organization. Robert Waterman, who might be considered as the primary popularizer of the state of the art in American managerial thought, writes:[35]

> High-performance companies differ from all the rest, I would say, in the ways in which they operate. In particular:
>
> - They are better organized to meet the needs of their employees, and they also attract people who are more effective than those of the competition. These people are more motivated to produce better work, whatever the job might be.
> - They are better organized to meet the needs of their customers, they are more innovative in anticipating customer needs, and better even at producing their goods and services at low cost, or any combination of these factors.

There are of course good reasons why one might question this best-of-all-possible-worlds optimism in which salaried employees, hourly employees and customers are reconciled. We will not defend this point of view here. But what stands out is the crucial role of the organization, in the sense of 'organizational arrangements', that is to say, not in terms of structure, but in the way in which people work, arrive at mutually satisfactory agreements, and co-operate more effectively and more actively. In particular, as we will see, bureaucracies are organizations which demand very little co-operation of their members. They in fact protect them from it, and in the case of the most strict organizations, they do away with co-operation altogether. This explains then the other aspect of the discussion of 'less' mentioned above: this 'less' strikes at the very heart of day-to-day concerns of the business place, on the relationship with others, on the need to share, to co-operate, in short, on all manner of behaviour which we will show is in no way spontaneous or natural.

This much deeper interpretation of the American situation is not meant to make any claims about its durability, its superiority or its success. We still lack sufficient perspective to pass judgement on the situation.[36] Nonetheless, our analysis helps show the extent to which in the 1990s the day-to-day affairs of the workplace are affected by this third industrial revolution. It allows us to formulate a first hypothesis, one which we will attempt to verify throughout this book: not only are executives no longer protected as once was possible, but today, they are all caught up together in the great tempest in which new organizations are being formed. They are the ones who feel the full force of what I call 'internal instability'.

Many words for a single disease

'Where is the world headed?' asked *Le Monde* columnist Erik Izraëlewicz in a recent article.[37] In exploring the alternatives, he contrasted the new economy, one which is built on regular growth and the creation of jobs as in the United States, with the other, which is the 'catastrophic approach', that of a great economic depression which has taken hold in France and part of Europe. And indeed, although one must take care not to confuse short-term phenomena with more serious trends, a survey of some of the titles which have appeared in the economic and social literature in France over the last decade is nothing short of striking: *L'horreur économique* (*Economic Horror*) of Viviane Forrester,[38] would certainly head the list, but what about *La concurrence et la mort* (*Competition and Death*) by Philippe Thureau-Dangin,[39] *Les peurs françaises* (*French Fears*) by Alain Duhamel,[40] *La France malade du travail* (*France Sick of Work*) by Jacques de Bandt, *et al.*[41] We would have no problem labelling the literature of this period 'morbid', an observation summed up rather nicely by the *International Herald Tribune* under the title 'A Somber France, Racked by Doubt'.[42]

These fears and uncertainties revolve around two main themes. The criticism of the idea that 'everything is of the market', and its consequences for human beings. Edgar Morin draws a brilliant comparison between liberalism and Satan, a rather nice metaphor for this trend.[43] Viviane Forrester echoes this theme from a literary and emotional perspective:

> time and time again it is the same phenomenon, that of the small group in power which no longer requires the labour of others (did we ever put them in charge of it?) who can get the hell out with all their uncertainties, their medical bulletins. But alas, there is nowhere else to go. At least not in this life, even for the faithful. There is no spare geography, no other ground to walk upon; these are the same lands, on the same planet, which from time immemorial go from garden to mass grave [44]

And whenever emotion gives way to analysis, the question which surfaces time and time again, in one work after another, is that of the end, the last drop of the 'always a little more' [45] which employees are asked to give, and which is in fact 'always a little less', as I argued earlier. In connection with the idea of flexibility, which we take to be sufficiently general so as to encompass the conditions under which one accepts employment (status of the employee, employee protection such as insurance and other benefits, retirement) as well as the conditions under which one works (schedules, job mobility, and also the organizations), the fear has broken out that this deterioration might be inescapable and that no compensation will be received in exchange. Even the technologies which accompany – or provoke – the breakdown, are viewed with suspicion.[46] Finally, there is, in the case of France, pressure from abroad imploring the nation to get moving, to 'give up' the idea of protecting itself.[47]

In fact, the rigidity of the French system as opposed to the adaptability of the Anglo-Saxon one, which is one way of characterizing the differences between these two approaches to the world, is indeed a matter which it might be worth taking a few steps back to re-examine.[48] But we can already suggest a hypothesis, which we will explore in more detail later on: French bureaucracies – including the French public administration which is at once the archetype and the model which the others have for a long time sought to imitate – are notorious for their skill at spontaneous adaptation, a skill which allows them to keep pace, as best as they can, with changes in the collective fabric in which they are caught up, but never to anticipate them.[49] These modes of adaptation – which include ways of bending the rules, the development of parallel networks linked to the *grands corps* which they are part of, and so on – appear today simply laughable, even counter-productive in light of the great leap which lies ahead. Above all, one precondition for their development was a context of abundant resources, a context which no longer exists today. As long as bureaucracies could 'buy' their customers, they survived and adapted. The day that they no longer have the means to do this, their deficiencies, their shortcomings, their excessive behaviour quickly become intolerable. The word 'adaptability' has taken on a new meaning, and the line of reasoning of the French bureaucrats provides them with no help in coping with these new realities.[50] In our view, this is why 'globalization' carries with it so much distress and fear: the consequences of globalization cannot be handled in the traditional French way.

Germany: in its own way

The case of Germany will allow us to expand our inventory of the general context in which the bureaucracy crisis is taking place. In Germany as in France the widespread Anglo-Saxon model of capitalism is not blindly accepted: 'Originally,' writes Alain Lebaube, 'there was nothing more opposed to the strategy of Anglo-Saxon capitalism, of globalization and flexibility than the centralized systems of the socio-democratic models which tend to standardize social relationships.'[51] This is no doubt why, when from the end of 1996 to the beginning of 1997, the unemployment rate in Germany went above the 12 per cent level. The worst fears of those who had predicted a crisis in the German model in its entirety were confirmed.[52] Some of the difficulties can be attributed to reunification,[53] but in the framework of this book, let us focus on three main points.

First of all, whatever the complex causes of the difficulties which Germany is experiencing – and no doubt there as everywhere they are piling up – the German economy is clearly industry-based, orientated towards production. Michel Drancourt makes the reasonable argument that 'for a long time Germans went along with the belief that by developing quality products, they could sell them at a high price, something which would permit a high level of remuneration and of social welfare'.[54] The choice between cost and quality is and will be each day less feasible. I will make the case in Part I that cost is not what stands in the way of satisfying the customer (this is the classic vision held by bureaucracies which always seek more means through which they might satisfy their customers), but the organization itself, in the sense of a mode of functioning, which will allow reconciling those things which once appeared irreconcilable. To oppose cost and quality – we will turn to the example of the impossible reform of French hospitals – is to maintain one's opposition to change at the customer's expense. At the same time, from the standpoint of change management, such a solution brings us right back to increases in physical production, unimaginative, brute, which can only heighten fear, increasing opposition and conflict.

From this angle, we arrive at the second point which surfaces in the case of Germany, that is to say, attempts to try to get out of this dilemma with something less than a full-blown crisis. We can learn a great deal from the rivalry between Renault and Volkswagen, regardless of how temporary this may be.[55] It shows that, despite the difficulties, helping technical bureaucracies get through these changes can be managed at a lower cost than was previously the case (Great Britain or even the United States), although the cost is still high in certain countries (France, for example).

A final noteworthy aspect of the German example – but one could say the same thing about Sweden – the bureaucratic crisis is also reaching, by a sort of ricochet effect, organizations which were traditionally grafted on to these bureaucracies, and fed off them. This is the case of the union movement. We noted earlier, along with Robert Reich, the decline of unions in America, although they are supposedly deeply rooted in the world of work and endowed with considerable means. With regard to this union myth, Jeremy Rifkin speaks of 'capitulation'.[56] Germany is no doubt undergoing something rather different: union activity has been and remains clearly much more institutionalized there than in the United States. Consequently, if the German model should implode, German unions might well implode along with it. Yet, this is not what we find, or at least not to such a degree. Union bureaucracies, like all bureaucracies, stand before a wall and must adapt[57] by reviewing the levels at which they can act (branch, business or institution), as well as the ways in which they can act (from global negotiation to attention given to special cases).

The need for change here does not stem directly from competition, it is rather the indirect consequence of environmental transformation. The main point of the foregoing is this: bureaucracies directly on the market or about to enter the market are not the only ones expected to die out. All forms of bureaucracy will be caught up in this contagious process. This book attempts to pinpoint just how this will happen.[58]

Asia: the dragons' frailty

Moving now to another stage in our discussion, let us take a look at some of the Asian countries (Japan, South Korea, China). The author had the opportunity to present an analysis of the 'Japanese miracle', highlighting the market more in terms of the system (its 'organization' in the sense that the word has been used here), than in terms of the miraculous recipes and other imaginary exaggerations which Western analysts have tried to import.[59] I identified, based upon the analysis of the white appliance industry, two explanatory facts which still seem today to be rather poorly understood: on one hand the roughly middle-aged organization of the Japanese distribution network, and on the other hand the power and remarkable harmony of their system of production. This system, largely organized into cartels, closely controls the widely dispersed distributors and dependent firms. These base-level units very rarely venture to offer foreign products, whatever the legal measures in place or however the authorities might object in good faith. The way in which the home market is dominated by producers, backed up by the financial control of consumer organizations, makes it possible to maintain a nucleus of loyal workers with guaranteed lifetime employment. This attachment is itself made possible by externalizing its cost on to part-time employees, hired to do their master's bidding. In the end, these are the employees for whom there is no sacred aura to the miracle.

In such a case, the problem of cost is not resolved through new techniques (Rifkin's hypothesis)[60] or through the organization as proposed in this book. It is resolved through pressure on the labour force. It certainly seems simple. But it is likely that the days are numbered for this competitive advantage. The strikes which occurred at the end of 1996 in South Korea drew attention to the social pressure which had been felt there since the 1980s and which now seems destined to reduce the advantages which that country once held.[61] The ongoing sluggishness of Japan, of great concern to Americans, could very well stem from the same source. It could even be suggested that China will follow more or less the very same path a little further down the road.[62]

So what can we draw from the foregoing? That in the end, the triumph of Japan, of South Korea, and perhaps yet tomorrow of China, have been, are, or will be only intermediate successes, their market advantage stemming only from a relatively inexpensive labour force? Those who believe in the end of work might add that 'it is only a question of time before this same labour force becomes useless'. Perhaps. But at least in an even shorter term the pressure on labour costs will not endure, first because developed countries will adapt to it either by reducing costs of their own labour force as they have already done, but more importantly by seeking their own increases in productivity in other forms of organization; second, because Asian countries will follow the same route, a route upon which the most developed of those countries have already set foot. With just a little imagination Western countries could manage to 'think the unthinkable' as suggested in this book, and those who have travelled to the East in search of a model might just turn around and head the other way.

Switzerland too!

Why conclude this introductory panorama with the case of Switzerland? One reason is that Switzerland is already well ahead of the pack in terms of globalization and the organizational revolution associated with it, as demonstrated by its international corporations such as Nestlé or ABB. Globalization is even one of their tools. Another reason is that throughout this introduction I have tried to underscore that the end of bureaucracies goes hand in hand with the end of certain aspects of social welfare, to put it very crudely. If there is one country in which the idea of social protection – against all: the world, pollution, conflict – is well established, it is in Switzerland. And yet, in the 1990s, this little country is subject to the very same constraints and thus the same uncertainties and fears as its more powerful neighbours. Stéphane Garelli, professor at the University of Lausanne notes that:

In fact, the country has two economies: a globalized economy, made up of international corporations which are extremely productive and open to the rest of the world, and then a local economy, one which is traditionally well-protected and expensive. Today, we are witnessing an increasingly widening dichotomy between the two: the globalized economy is doing well and is being restructured, whereas the local economy is suffering and stagnating.[63]

There as elsewhere, everything which humans have invented to avoid the tribulations of confronting others – co-operation, as we have already seen – is now brought into question. But for once it is worth being clear on this point: this is not about traditional forms of social welfare, acquired by possessing a certain status: these are but one particular kind and clearly not the most important in the case of Switzerland. Rather, I am referring to the situations of relative comfort at work which traditional organizations have little by little created for their members, and which today are crumbling. The Swiss example leads to another dimension which will be illustrated in this work. Bureaucracy, as will be defined later on, has nothing to do with the size of the organization in question. No doubt the protected Swiss economy at stake here is quite unlike the tentacular monsters of the French or Italian public school systems, for example. Simply put, the revolution of organizations is unavoidable, it has begun everywhere we turn. Like a steamroller, this revolution is reaching all countries and all collective forms of the production of goods and services, regardless of size, status or any other considerations.

Why organizations?

This book suggests therefore that even if globalization is the key factor, we can focus our analysis on its consequences on organizations (businesses or administrations). It is hoped that the presentation will assist general readers as well as specialists to understand the direction in which organizations are moving, and to identify where exactly there is room to manoeuvre. The problem of direction which the author has dealt with over the past few years in seminars held with executives is nothing short of amazing. It seems that the necessity of change is no longer a point of contention: it has become part and parcel of the rhetoric of modern times. But when we wish to know why we must change, most only mutter a few words or remain silent. Certainly, the less direction there is, the less we understand problems: it is then all the more difficult to come up with solutions, to accept them, and to put them into practice.

If we chose to view organizations from this standpoint, it is also because of a historical observation: all technological revolutions, even today, are accompanied by organizational revolutions. We will return to Taylorism in this work, and claim that it is an organizational revolution, no doubt still incomplete. But there is no reason why we should today be exempt from this rule. The explosion of technologies of all kinds is once again going to overturn the situation of men and women at work. These are some of the issues that will be explored here, through the use of simple concepts and case studies which will help explain better the observations and concepts set forth.

The concepts offered here will be simple, since reality is complex. This again is an issue on which many authors agree. We must think differently in order to understand, and, if possible, to have some control over reality. As I said before, we must 'think the unthinkable', otherwise the unthinkable will be thought by someone else and will take place anyway, painfully and tragically, especially since it will be misunderstood.

The book is divided into two parts. Part I will be devoted to reasons *why*: Why must organizations change, and in particular, those organizations which we call bureaucracies? What does the customer require of the bureaucrat? The problem of meaning mentioned earlier will be of interest here. Part II will focus on the *how* of change: What tools (intellectual or methodological) do we have at our disposal which might allow us to keep pace with change, or just to keep the human cost as low as possible?

Notes

1. Cf. Chapter 1.
2. See, for example, Waterman (1995).
3. Morin and Naïr (1997), p. 194.
4. *Ibid.*
5. Forrester (1996).
6. Castel (1995). Note that this extremely well-documented book provides a useful and fruitful way of looking at all that has been said and written about work in general and salaried employment in particular.
7. Rifkin (1996), p. 117.
8. Morin and Naïr. (1997), p. 89.
9. On the United States, see Leseman (1988). On Great Britain, see Ville (1994). These works are cited by Robert Castel.
10. It is true that one has to work with some of the huge public or para-public French monsters to find even today weak union organizations, artificially maintained in a dominant role by management since the 'fear of social concerns' has a strong impact on company strategy.
11. Reich (1992), p. 6.
12. Castel (1995), p. 436.

13. Jean-Marie Thievenard in Laroche (1997).
14. For a quick review of the literature concerning this debate, see *Le Monde Economie*, 28 January 1997.
15. Crozier (1994).
16. Much of the executive class at the time thought that France could escape the widespread paralysis and its consequences thanks to the strength of its agricultural sector.
17. Tofler (1991).
18. This is moreover a noteworthy reversal. Robert Castel (1995) shows that for many centuries, within the Catholic tradition, outcasts were not really a constraint for the wealthy, but rather a resource.
19. Morin and Naïr (1997), p. 100.
20. Dear to Jeremy Rifkin (1996) in particular Chapter 17, 'Renforcer le tiers secteur', pp. 328–57. For France, see the preface written by Michel Rocard for this book, pp. i–xvii. This is also a theme of which Jacques Delors is very fond.
21. See for example the analysis presented by Sami Naïr in Morin and Naïr (1997).
22. One example of this can be found in the slightly different but mostly very optimistic analysis of Jean-Paul Fitoussi and Pierre Rosanvallon (1996).
23. Cf. the second part of this book.
24. This term was popularized by Michael Hammer and James Champy (1993). On p. 40 the authors write: 'If we had to define re-engineering of a company in a few words, we would offer the following, "to start from scratch." Re-engineering... does not involve reworking what already exists, no more than modifying for an nth time some system without getting at its fundamental structure. It is not redistributing existing systems in the hope of getting them to run more smoothly... Reconfiguring a business means getting rid of previous systems and starting over.'
25. Harnel and Prahalad (1994). See also de Bandt (1997) and de Bandt and de Bandt-Flouriol (1996).
26. Morin and Naïr (1997).
27. Rifkin (1996), especially the second part 'La troisième révolution industrielle', and the third 'Le déclin mondial du travail', pp. 93–226.
28. Which is by the way the main point discussed by Robert Reich (1992).
29. Rifkin (1996), Ch. 5 'La technologie et l'expérience des noirs américains', pp. 106–20.
30. Marti (1997).
31. *New York Times*, (1993), p. 15; *Training* (1993). Cited in Rifkin (1996), pp. 229–33.
32. Reich (1992), p. 7.
33. Rifkin (1996), p. 230.
34. We will return to this concept at the beginning of Part II.
35. Waterman (1995), p. 17.
36. See, for example, Lampière (1997).
37. Izraëlewicz (1997c).
38. Forrester (1996).
39. Thureau-Dangin (1995).
40. Duhamel (1993).
41. De Bandt *et al.* (1995).
42. Cohen (1997).
43. Edgar Morin writes that 'Religious fundamentalism, ethnic nationalism and differentialism are at once the manifestation of conservatism and the dark side of liberalism erected in a system for the world. Be this as it may, one Satan cannot take the place of another. Liberalism is not responsible for everything... It is just that

its radical victory engenders its radical reverse side. And it is a reverse side headed in a backward direction.' (Morin and Naïr (1997), p. 194).

44. Forrester (1996), p. 57.
45. See, for example, Lebaube (1997a): 'Whereas companies have obtained everything they want, they continue to demand the easing of restrictions. Just how far can they go?'
46. See, for example, 'Société en réseau', *Libération* (1997a).
47. Kapstein (1997). The author, professor of political economics at the University of Minnesota, writes: 'European leaders are in the process of tackling the problem of welfare benefits, as much within as outside their own borders...In fact, the crisis of European public finance gives each government the chance to reform the social contract which binds it to its citizens.'
48. See, in the same issue of *Le Monde* (4 March 1997) the article by Henriot:(1997) The author states that out of 959 000 net jobs created between 1986 and 1996, 'three-fourths are either of a short-term nature, are temporary jobs, or paid internships', reminding us of the words of Robert Reich and Jeremey Rifkin concerning the United States.
49. Dupuy and Thoenig (1985). See also *Le Monde Emploi* which follows the same line of thinking as the former, but appears 11 years later.
50. Crozier (1995).
51. Lebaube (1997b).
52. For example, Gave (1996) and Milano (1996).
53. *Libération* (1997b).
54. Drancourt (1997).
55. *Le Monde* (1997b).
56. Rifkin (1996), p. 154.
57. Cf. *Le Monde Emploi* (1997b).
58. An interesting example are the two major labour unions in France: the CGT (Conféderation générale du travail) associated with the Communist Party, and the CFDT (Conféderation française démocratique du travail). The infamous economic crisis in France provided opportunity for the CFDT, which underwent transformation, but was taken poorly by the CGT, which has been particularly resistant to change.
59. Dupuy and Thoenig (1986).
60. Rifkin (1996), p. 195. Rifkin writes: 'New technology is starting to make the clothing industry of the industrialized nations just as competitive as the manufacturing companies of the low-wage nations. As manufacturing processes begin to bow to reconfiguration and automation, even exporters from the third world countries such as China or India will be forced to shift from the current methods requiring a large labour force, to the faster and more cost-effective techniques of mechanized production.'
61. Chaponnière (1997).
62. See Izraëlewicz (1997b).
63. Garelli (1997).

Part I

THE PROBLEM

The Customer's Victory and Consequences for Organizations

1 The Organization, Concreteness, Complexity

Part I will focus on how organizations are affected by the 'customer's victory' which is another and simple way to translate 'globalization'. This is not to say that we will enter into the debate on how corporate structures could adapt to a more competitive marketplace, or discuss the beneficial effects of matrix-like organization as opposed to vertical companies, nor even the virtues of centralization in light of the problems which can be caused by excessive decentralization. This would be to return to the familiar debate on types of organizational structure, a debate which, beginning with Taylor, occupies an important place in the literature. Ever since Henri Mintzberg's seminal work,[1] 'structure' has consistently been a topic of great interest.[2] Some even consider structural change to be the mainspring, the cornerstone of organizational change.[3]

Organization is not structure

It is the author's view that, as interesting as it is, debate masks the more important factors, side-stepping the real problem. Only when a clear distinction is made between organization and structure – and, hopefully, is clearly understood – can we begin to appreciate the extent of changes about to take place or already underway in both private companies and public administration. We will try to understand better why the confusion between organization and structure keeps coming back to the forefront of discussion. The reason for this is in part intellectual: reality – that is, the concrete way in which organizations function, in which employees work, co-operate and resolve their problems, and so on – can be frightening. We will return to this point. But there is also a practical reason: if change – even the most basic kind of change – can be reduced to modifications of the organizational chart, to the movement of 'boxes', functions, of responsibilities, to links to new managers, or, in short, to development of automatic, mechanized processes like these, then things are relatively easy.

Yet based on what earlier specialists called the formal and the informal,[4] it seemed that a clear distinction had been made. Let us go back to an article by Waterman *et al.* dating from 1980. Under a simple title, one which would work well on the cover of the present volume, *Organization is Not Structure*,[5] the authors write:

> The Belgian surrealist René Magritte painted a series of pipes entitled *This is not a pipe*. An object depicted on canvas is not the object. Similarly, a structure is not an organization. We all know this, yet as we reorganize, we are often in fact only restructuring, as though there were no real difference.
>
> All managers and consultants know intellectually that an organization extends far beyond official charts, boxes, hierarchical lines, descriptions of operations, or matrices. Yet we behave as though we did not know it. If we want to change, we change structure.

It has all been said before, but must be said again:

> The organizational models which have been used until now seem to fall short in describing business realities and the management of these realities. Existing models borrow heavily from the imagery of physics (which concerns inanimate objects) or from military or administrative practices, and describe environments which are not very complex or dynamic.[6]

These two passages have much in common, despite the 17 years that separate them.

Thus there are good reasons for reconsidering the distinction between structure and organization in an attempt to understand why these concepts have been confused for so long. Drawing a simple example from my work in seminars, it is interesting to note that time and time again one can observe an apparent contradiction in discussions held with business executives, regardless of their cultural background. Concerning the idea that organizations do not operate according to their own rules and procedures – and that, moreover, if they did, they would be unable to function at all – not only do they all agree, but they provide plenty of examples to illustrate the point. They observe for instance that each language has its own way to express the avoidance of rules: in France it is called *tourner la règle*, in Britain and America *to bend* or *to break the rules*. Yet, when asked to describe their own organization, they immediately turn to the official chart and most often go no further. Backed into a corner, they are perfectly willing to talk about 'individuals' and their psychological or physical characteristics (age, sex and so on), but they are inevitably stymied by the question 'How does it all work?', that is, by reality. By invoking official charts and procedures, they feel as though they are being concrete since they are speaking about what is visible and immediately visualizable.

This then is the first area of confusion: there is good reason to look into what is really 'concrete', even if the answer to this question might lead us to complexity. The press has helped spread the misconception that something is concrete only when it can be seen and understood in a physical way. Taken to an extreme – as is often done – this idea can lead to the belief that the use of thought processes and concepts on one hand and concreteness on the other are contradictory. The query, 'Could you explain that in concrete terms?', so often heard in televised debates, brings out numbers, statistics and anecdotes, but not the facts; simplism and not complexity; that which is seen but not understood. In short, confusion between appearance and reality, and, in respect to change, between the problem and the symptom.

It is important to see that in so doing, we are fooling ourselves, labelling 'concrete' what is in fact very abstract. In the state of Indiana, for example, as in several American states, there is a law against the sale of alcohol on Sunday, even though studies have shown Sunday to be the day on which people imbibe the most. What can be more abstract than that? In respect to organizations, what can be more abstract than when, in a traditional bureaucracy, workshop supervisors or executives are told, 'You are the boss' (hierarchical power), without giving them control over any of the factors necessary to gain the co-operation of those whom they are supposed to lead?[7] There have even appeared, as a result of this confusion, what we might call 'virtual organizations'.[8] Built upon structures which only distantly represent the real ways in which they function, based on statistics (market possibilities for example) which reveal little more than the information which those who are in touch with this market think they should reveal, virtual organizations quickly set up a 'reporting' system, a way of controlling management, and human resource management systems, which 'churn out' numbers, measures and forecasts which have little to do with the real world. In the end, what we have here is little more than the well-worn principle that bureaucracies are always able to invent that which justifies their own activities. And, when you ask those organizations, which have acquired an amazing ability to toss and turn in a vacuum, about reality – 'What really is going on?' – you are immediately suspected of over-complicating matters. This too is a significant paradox, allowing us to see where the problem lies: concreteness is supposed to be simple, when in fact, reality is complex.

Concreteness, at least for organizations, is something altogether different.[9] Let us use the following practical definition: it is the set of strategies which the actors – either individuals or groups – develop as they begin to interrelate about solving their problems, in so doing mobilizing resources and facing constraints. There are two implications here.

The first is that 'the concrete' is what the actors do rather than what they ought to do (rules and procedures). In this respect, it is important to note that change is not so much the modification of structures or procedures, but the modification of 'strategies', or, put more simply, of the actors' behaviour. We will return to this point in the following section.

The second – and this is crucial again in view of managing change – is that official charts, the rules and so on, are part of the actors' context (what we have called resources and constraints). Consequently, they can be used as levers to introduce some change into the system, provided that we have grasped their systemic dimension (actors use them, play with them), and not just their linear dimension (actors behave just as the charts and rules predict they should).[10] Here is an example to help illustrate this point. It concerns a complex system in which the rules wind up producing effects that are exactly opposite to those expected: the public system of ground transport carriers in France, as it stood a few years ago.[11]

The public transportation system in France

In fact a good starting point for the analysis of the ground carrier industry is to consider what happens whenever the loaders – those who have something to transport – do not make the delivery themselves but turn to a specialized surface carrier.

Traditionally, the authorities – and in this case officials at the Direction des Transports Terrestres, part of the French Transportation Ministry – make use of what we have called linear vision. In their eyes, the number one problem in the industry is that the carriers, independent or self-employed, commit fraud by breaking the rules.[12] This is understandable. Ever since the nationalization of the French railroads in 1936, the entire ground transport system has been subject to detailed, finical regulation, covering or having covered virtually all aspects of operations, from the very ability to provide services (long-haul transport licences), to the 'social' conditions of the carrier business (how long drivers can be at the wheel, how long they must rest and so on), including pricing regulations (an obligatory transport pricing scale, or OTP, existed for a long time, setting for each potential shipment a price ceiling and floor). Finally, in addition to the laws and bylaws of France, there are those of the European Union.

With this line of thinking, government officials highlight statistics in support of the idea that fraud causes accidents (drivers who fall asleep at the wheel, for example): getting carriers to abide by the rules is therefore in the public's best interest. In this way, these officials manage to convince the representative in charge of the carriers (the Minister) to do something. The Minister knows that the transportation industry is a sensitive one: we do not have to look far to find an example of its ability to paralyse the economy of an entire nation, which is precisely what happened in France in 1992 and again in 1997. Similar events have occurred in other countries, such as Chile. For this reason, the Minister takes a pragmatic view of the problem, acting only if there will be some real advantage for constituents, in this instance a significant reduction in traffic accidents.

But what is the best way to tackle the problem? This is where linear reasoning comes in, avoiding the complexity of the problem. If carriers commit fraud, slipping through loopholes in regulation, it is because the rules are too lax. They must therefore be tightened, in this case, by increasing in some concrete way the regulation of truck drivers – a good example of which is the driver's licence based on a point system, introduced in France in 1992 – and then to increase control measures, without which regulation would have no effect, since we are talking here about people who, in the eyes of government officials, could not care less about the rules. This example, albeit a bit exaggerated here, clearly shows that for the government official, 'transport', which we intend to analyse here as a complex system, is reduced to one simple operation, the movement of goods – and to one lead actor – the truck drivers, who would escape unnoticed if they did not break the rules. Yet, if we take a look at how the problem is then affected by the strategy employed – more rules and more control measures – the situation is nothing short of bleak: truckers break the rules with increasing frequency, which requires new rules, until the day when the entire situation blows up, if only because the vicious circle has become so tight that it must be broken.

Is there another way of looking at the situation, one that is less simplistic and more effective? The answer is yes, provided that we are willing first to tackle the issue of complexity, and second if we are willing to go back into the field and listen to those involved, that is, try to understand 'how it all works'. Here is an illustration: if a truck is carrying merchandise, it is because someone has goods to be shipped. We called this person the loader. The loaders can either work directly with a carrier, quite often what we might call a 'large carrier' (we will get back to this label later on) or, they can work though a third party – known within the business by various names: an auxiliary, a grouper, a forwarding agent, a shipping agent – who is the true specialist both of the rules of the trade, familiar with the intricacies of the network, and able to bring together supply and demand. This is the person who can fill a partially empty truck as it heads out and bring it back with a full load.

Note as well that subcontracting is widespread throughout the business. The 'large carriers' are thereby able to transfer a contract to smaller and perhaps less well-equipped firms, just as shipping agents can choose the companies they deal with depending on the kind of work requested. To summarize briefly: we have gone beyond the simplistic view which focused only on the truck driver, and are now dealing with at least four different actors: the loader, the shipping agent, the large carrier and the small carrier. For the sake of completeness, we should also include the French National Railways (the SNCF) which is the country's number one surface freight carrier, the various inspectors who keep a close eye on the industry, and the different branches of management related to equipment, working conditions and the like, which churn out the rules, provide documentation and sometimes even run inspections.

Let us take yet another step towards complexity by considering two factors: first, the pressure on pricing. In the days of the OTP, most transactions took place at the lowest rate, if not unofficially below that. Since its elimination, the *de facto* situation has not really changed. This is clear evidence that within the system, what is scarce is not the means of transportation, but the freight. Whosoever controls this scarcity – this uncertainty – is the one with the real power. In the present case, it is either the loader, the shipping agent or the large carriers who turn to subcontractors: these three have in common that they are not involved in driving the trucks, and so are not direct targets of regulation.[13] It is quite a remarkable paradox that linear reasoning places blame on the least powerful actors in the game, simply because they are 'visible', disregarding those who are really in control. This is what is called here 'false concreteness', confusion between appearance and reality.

Second, let us consider why the loader might choose to work through a shipping company. Why do more companies not handle shipping in-house, especially in a country like France, which has always held middlemen responsible for many of its problems? To get to the bottom of this, we must view the problem from the loaders' perspective: they feel pressure from both above and below. From above, there is pressure related to production, which is under increasing strain, happening more and more 'just in time', leading to the last-minute delivery of orders. From below, the loaders are faced with customers who similarly wish to avoid large product stockpiles, hoping to acquire the merchandise only as it is needed out on the showroom floor. Now, if we add to these pressures those which arise from the regulation of the ground carrier industry, it is obvious that everyone cannot be satisfied. As expected, loaders focus on their own problems, on their relationship with customers, and they will outsource with specialists – carriers or shipping agents – as business requires. To put it bluntly, their carriers will have to be flexible, that is, ready to commit fraud. If not directly, then indirectly, since the owner of the shipping company will require his or her own employees to commit fraud, which amounts to the same thing. Does this mean that the whole business is corrupt? Of course not, since loaders require 'flexibility' in perhaps only 1 per cent of all cases; the ability of the carrier to say 'yes' at a given moment depends a great deal on the possibility that they will have that customer on a regular basis, in a business environment in which, as we saw earlier, what is scarce is the freight.

Let us continue just a little further along the path of 'concreteness'. Assuming that the loader's requirements are complex, implying that rules are being broken regularly, and that transactions do not involve a lot of profit. Large carriers can quickly decide to accept an offer, for the reasons mentioned above, without running the risk of having to deliver in-house. They can subcontract to smaller firms, the 'small carriers'. This label has nothing to do with the number of trucks a carrier owns: the small carrier is the one which operates its own vehicles – or one of a fleet of vehicles – and which therefore is not necessarily available for a particular business endeavour, relying entirely on others to locate freight for it. It will receive its contracts either directly through shipping agents, or through subcontract arrangements with larger carriers – which, for their part, are not 'stuck behind the wheel'. What the small carrier winds up with, you have guessed it, is the hot potato: fraud. The less free the small carrier is, the more likely it will accept such deals even when profits are low, everyone else having taken a cut.

What can be said? That, viewed as a system, carrier fraud is not a problem, but a solution. It is what marketing specialists call a 'differential advantage', in a world in which companies fight it out to get freight. In such an environment, tightening regulation on the weakest players only deprives them of some of the elbow room which they have to work in, so to speak, limiting their ability to make real choices. They spoke out against this in July of 1992, when the weakest ones, both salaried and self-employed drivers, brought France's highways to a standstill, simply to say that they could not drive any slower.[14]

One more thing. Having grasped the idea of a 'system of ground transport' – the system of concrete action of Crozier and Friedberg – which is very different from the simplistic view of the movement of goods from place to place, we are faced with the question of cost. Everything revolves around the breaking of rules – which in fact regulates the system from a sociological standpoint – but fraud comes at a high price: accidents. Can something be done about this? It is time to identify yet another key player, an important one, who up till now has gone unnoticed: the insurance company, which, in its analyses of risk, makes no special provisions for trucks. The insurance company is the instrument through which the expense of breaking the rules in an attempt to regulate the system of ground transport is projected on to all French motorists.

From this point on, change can be analysed in a systemic rather than a linear fashion. For example, whenever there are damages caused by an accident in which a truck is at fault, why not implicate the entire chain of command and not just the truck driver, as has been done in France since the movement of 1992? Why not mutualize the truck risk, so to speak, based on the English model, reintegrating within the system the costs of this mode of functioning, modifying the context so that it can function differently, less expensively, and thus with less fraud? A paradox of complexity: formal logic could find itself reversed in favour of reasoning which is perhaps less 'simple' to formulate, but which is much more concrete with respect to accounting for reality. We can substitute false common sense which tells us 'since accidents are caused by fraud, then if we cut down on infractions of trucking laws, we will reduce the number of accidents', with the following process: 'by making the cost of an accident so great that the entire ground transport system cannot bear it, we can reduce fraud, which is precisely what causes cost overruns'. In short, now that reality has been grasped, let us reduce accidents so as to cut down on fraud!

These two types of reasoning are represented schematically in Figures 1.1 and 1.2.

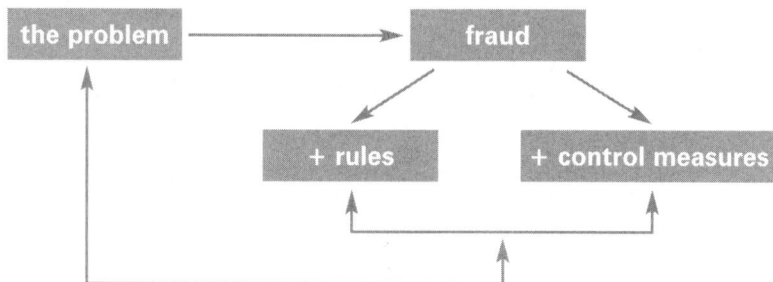

Figure 1.1   Linear and causal reasoning

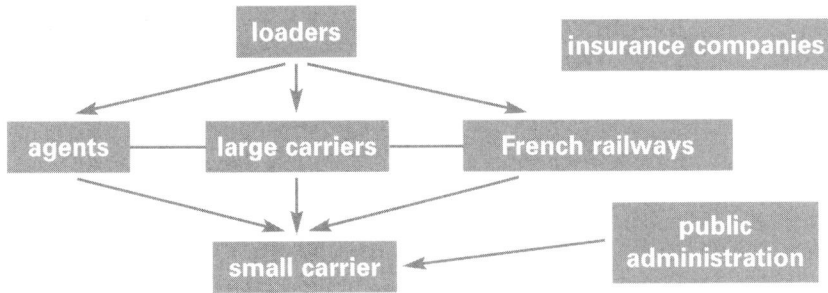

Figure 1.2   Systemic and complex reasoning

Thus, complexity and simplicity are not contradictory, no more than complexity and concreteness. They are different only insofar as we cease to think about them clearly, mistaking appearance (Magritte's pipes) for reality, the only reality which can be meaningful for employees within an organization and which should have meaning for their superiors. It is very common that within businesses, in company meetings, and as companies make decisions, people refuse to deal in terms of the concrete, returning over and over to abstractness. Companies help protect everyone involved – 'I made a decision, I changed structure' – without requiring anyone to face up to the reality of the situation, without even having to discuss it, for that is far more complicated and perceived to be far more dangerous.

The paradox of the executive

Reality – concreteness – is frightening, and it is most frightening for those in charge. Of course, it has been said over and over that the way in which our leaders are educated certainly does not predispose them to see it. In France, the technical or managerial *grandes ecoles* focus mostly on technical aspects. In the United States, immediately following college graduation, and even in the best business schools, abstract models tend to replace any real attempts at understanding reality. This has been the trend in American schools during these last three decades of the century.

But there is more. For those in charge, reality is seen as a threat. They are thus determined to face it only as a last resort, when forced to do so. But why is reality a threat? No doubt because reality exposes each person as he or she really is, revealing to the entire organization how weak the leaders actually are, how small their impact is in fact on the course of events, and, lastly, how heavily they rely on others to get by. Remember that organizations and especially bureaucracies are systems of inverted power. The leaders rely more on the subordinates than the subordinates on the leaders. Brought to light, these fundamental facts of corporate life would greatly affect the behaviour of leaders. On one hand, it would force them to take a more modest view of their own role in the organization: in our prevailing models, the leader is supposed to know just about everything, even to be able to make decisions for the common good. It is very difficult for leaders to admit that the 'emperors wear no clothing', that is, to concretely face up to their situations. And yet in such a case, what we call modesty is simply admitting that reality, since it is complex, cannot be globally transformed, even and especially by the supreme leaders. Just like everyone else, they are confronted with the problem of 'elbow room' in which to manoeuvre, which is no greater for them than for anyone else. In the second part of this book we will return to this notion and outline a strategy for managing change.

Confronted with this situation, the leader instinctively shifts blame for fearing to face reality on to everyone else. 'Would not it be dangerous to show those people the true face of things? How could they accept it?' To this question, it has become the author's regular practice to answer company leaders with a question of his own: 'If you do not want to talk to them about reality, what do you talk to them about, day in and day out?' The answer is clear: businesses are always talking about abstract ideas taken from statistics, surveys, opinion and attitude polls; about culture, leadership and all kinds of prescriptive data related to behaviour, but which have no bearing on real-life situations.

And yet, reality could have its place. My studies and those of other researchers show that, so long as it is done without assigning blame, members of an organization are both ready and able to discuss concreteness, even more so than their leader. They probably do not hold the same abstract ideas about what should be and what in fact is not. This is what we call 'the leaders' paradox': the less they are able to control reality, the more they think that others share their fears.

For the same reason and through the same mechanisms, decisions always take priority over problems.[15] As it is, making decisions is not easy, and overall, within organizations people have spent more energy in devising ways to avoid decisions than in actually making them: backed into a corner they prefer familiar well-defined solutions, even if those solutions have nothing to do with the problem. This can be illustrated with an anecdote. In 1997, the author had the opportunity to participate in a long work session with the executive committee of one of the largest individual French groups. The CEO had summoned everyone for an important announcement: the decision had just been made to decentralize the group worldwide. Quite impressive. A discussion ensued over how decentralization would be carried out, each contributor stressing his or her own model, his or her own solution. Finally, the sacrilegious question: 'Why do you want to decentralize?' at which point a disapproving hush fell over the meeting, and the CEO, obviously annoyed, blurted out, 'Because we are too centralized!' Despite the heavy atmosphere, a series of specific questions regarding the facts and employee behaviour revealed little by little that the organization had lost control of the decentralized units, and that, consequently, the real problem was that there was far too much autonomy, the local units rarely reporting back to the centre. Controlling this autonomy would no doubt have consisted in both centralizing and decentralizing depending on what level within the organization one is at, and according to the concrete mechanisms and results of these mechanisms which would be brought to light by a careful analysis of reality. A few words from the consultant who had just been hired to help manage the decentralization process brought the entire issue to a dead halt right then and there.

The fear of social issues

The point here, which goes against the leading – and perhaps only – way of thinking in the field of management today, is that reality is tough to face up to because understanding it is difficult, and often requires a great deal of effort.[16] It is one of the great paradoxes of concreteness that it is so hard to see with the naked eye;[17] it is therefore easy to confuse the symptom with the problem, and to focus on visible individual behaviour which it is believed can be modified at will by the individuals in question. The real organization – the system – remains concealed. As we have come to see, the problem is not with the symptom, but with the problem itself,[18] however unusual the turn of phrase may seem! Let us consider an illustration of this, which will also serve to introduce the following chapter on the consequences of the customer's victory over the organization.

During a particularly bad winter storm, a large European railroad company was unable to handle the increase in traffic. Trains were stopped for hours in open country, passengers were unable to get out of freezing, inhospitable stations, and worst of all, they received virtually no information on the situation from company employees. Some employees had left to assist engineers on the trains, or had gone home, saying that their work day was over. Well, the news media got hold of the issue, and raised it to a level of national concern, which eventually led the president of the company to appear on television saying that his employees had done the best they could. This of course only worsened the relationship between the company and its customers. Yet, after the ordeal was over, the company decided to open a task force on employees' attitudes concerning customer service.

By linking their problems to employee 'attitudes', company directors pointed an accusing finger at the guilty party – employees who interact with customers – setting them apart from the rest of the organization. This of course is to grossly oversimplify the matter. According to company directors, employees were like misbehaving children and simply needed to 'change their attitude', as if it were a question of willpower, or of good-will! This is clearly oversimplistic and guilt-provoking.

Upon closer inspection, several facts help to understand the problem in its full proportions, and thus open the way to an entirely different, concrete approach to the quality of customer service. First, there are many company employees working directly with customers, and they form a highly varied group. There are sales agents, conductors, receptionists, each with different backgrounds, different working conditions (on board or in the stations), and are linked to the company through different channels (be it through a hierarchical structure or through professional organizations). These employees form formidable fortresses, at least as viewed by company management which is terrified at the prospect of upsetting them, always putting off until tomorrow open dialogue with them, and so the status quo continues in a kind of vicious circle. Overall, the organization is divided into many parts with a strong hierarchical dimension, resulting in the politicization of the groups, each one defending its own territory. Moreover, the 'powers from above' have a damping effect on any changes which are attempted, more or less stifling them in spite of the good intentions of those involved.

The modes of functioning – what we call here the real organization – are built around two factors which seemingly cannot be avoided or even questioned: technical constraints and safety. The customer is kept on the outside of the organization, and 'customer advising', as we said, depends wholly on the goodwill of company representatives. These employees are never required to redefine their own job descriptions so as to work with the customer's agenda and provide quality service as the customer sees it. That would require understanding two complex dimensions: first, that the employee working with the customer is a kind of 'last link' in the company chain. His or her behaviour cannot be understood in isolation, nor modified without modifying the entire organization of which he or she is only one part. Second, caught within this chain, there is much more involved in a given employee's daily interactions with customers than courtesy or 'communication'. To grasp this point, let us compare two situations.

In situation A, trains are brought to a standstill by bad weather. Here the customer's complaint is unrelated to the actual technical difficulties of maintaining rail service. Rather, the passenger is upset about the lack of information, the company's unwillingness to 'be there', ready to talk. The company retorts: 'We did what we could' – technically no one doubts that – 'and we said everything we knew, that is to say, very little' – which is probably the result of the chain effect pointed out above. Clearly in this instance 'attitudes' are not defined in terms of customer expectations – 'Tell me what you know, tell me what you do not know, but at least share with me your knowledge or ignorance' – but in terms of what the company thinks is 'logical', 'reasonable' or 'rational' to reveal.

In situation B, an aeroplane is stranded on the runway of an American airport. Here the crisis is handled differently, and the differences are independent of the individual employees involved. The standstill is the same, due to weather conditions at the destination, something which customers cannot directly observe. What is more, customers are imprisoned in the plane since everyone had to board so that the pilots could be ready to take off as soon as technically possible; at the same time, customers cannot get out, since the plane left the boarding ramp, freeing it up for other planes on account of heavy air traffic. Because the chain co-operates altogether differently, there arises between the plane's technical crew and flight attendants actual dialogue rather than stereotyped, standardized, preconceived information unrelated to the customer's concerns. The crew informs passengers of the nature of the problem – weather conditions at the point of arrival – and speculates on how long they will have to wait, emphasizing that the guess is sketchy at best. While waiting for departure, the crew provides regular updates, telling passengers what they know, even sharing their own doubts. At the same time, on-board personnel assist passengers with their connections – especially those that will be missed – putting them in touch with personnel on the ground, seeking 'live' solutions to problems.

In short, without painting the first situation all black, nor glorifying the second, we have here two opposing ways of handling the relationship with the customer, corresponding to two different organizations, and not to two different types of individuals. In the case of the railroad company, the result is deep misunderstanding between management and employees.

Management does not understand the complexity of the situation. It is a dialogue of the deaf! For company representatives, even though they might not state it exactly in these terms, 'attitudes' are linked to their own situation within the organization – statutory, hierarchical – and their technical understanding of a problem. For those in management, these attitudes correspond to individual behaviour, which employees could change if they wanted to. In such a context, there is little use examining the pros and cons of common sense or of an economic rationale.

The other problem – lack of understanding – relates to what is really at stake in a change of 'attitude': which is all the more difficult to see since the very word is inappropriate. As we have seen, employee behaviour is built upon an endogenous rationale, that is, one which is concerned with technical criteria or job security, and with an understanding of the customer's needs. The employee derives from this a job, and develops a way of doing things at work which offers quite a bit of protection from pressure, especially pressure from the customer, and a great deal of autonomy in his or her daily life. By autonomy are meant the things which make the work environment more comfortable, as well as the settlements or deals which employees come up with themselves and which also constitute part of what we are calling the organization: employees' real work schedules, substitutions on the trains, the policy of going home as soon as a particular task is finished ('when you're done, you leave'), and so on. Company leaders openly claim to be unaware of this side of reality. And yet this is the only side that counts: as long as the relationship between the customer and the company representative is formed around technical concerns in the largest sense, the employees are the ones who control the relationship, imposing their view of the situation, their pace, their constraints. To take on 'attitudes' related to customer service is to act as if this reality does not exist: the concrete aspects are missing. It is obvious then that because they do not understand the real organization, managers do not know what to do, dithering over the possible consequences of their actions.

Organization and concreteness cannot be clearly defined because reality cannot be clearly defined, a fact which must be accepted. To be concrete is to sometimes accept vagueness. Any attempt to eliminate this vagueness through models or official charts, *a priori* analyses, or to try to blame it on an individual – either a guilty employee or leader – is to oversimplify the matter. To do so may not have dire consequences provided that the market is strong: an abundance of resources tends to minimize the consequences of being out of touch with reality, of abstractness. An abundance of means can reabsorb whatever might be lost in terms of cost or quality. This probably explains why bureaucracies are first and foremost systems of distribution. But as soon as this market trend is permanently destabilized, it becomes increasingly difficult to get by in a virtual world, if only because it is less possible to force others to bear the cost of such behaviour. As the third party slips away, the principles of reality take hold. This then is what organizations must confront as the twentieth century draws to a close. Let us see why.

Notes

1. Mintzberg (1982).
2. See, for example the analysis presented in Hammer and Champy (1993), pp. 15–40; 'Le taylorisme dépassé mais jamais remplacé', in Francfort *et al.* (1995), pp. 49–98; Zarifian (1993); or the classic, Lawrence and Lorsch (1986).
3. See, for example, Nadler *et al.* (1992).
4. Roethlisberger and Dikson (1939).
5. Waterman *et al.* (1980).
6. Bergmann and Uwaminger (1997), p. 344.
7. The management of uncertainty is the more exact term; see Crozier (1964).
8. See in Chapter 7, the case of the 'European Bank of Development'.
9. We are making explicit reference here to the concept of a 'system of concrete action', the importance and originality of which has no doubt not been fully understood. For a precise and truly convincing description of this, see Crozier and Friedberg (1990).
10. On the 'systemic' use of rules, we refer the reader to Friedberg (1993).
11. This example appeared originally in Dupuy and Thoenig (1979).
12. Today, the problem which we face is phrased in different words. For an updating of these case studies see Ocqueteau and Thoenig (1997).
13. At least before 1992/1993.
14. See Dupuy (1992).
15. Refer to Crozier (1995), the first to make explicit this observation.
16. See in Part II, Chapter 6 on a 'frame of reference'.
17. This 'naked emperor' effect, that of an accumulation of fear in the face of reality and of the difficulty to control it, has been clearly underscored by Chris Agyris. He writes: 'Thus, from the moment when the quest for continuous improvement got professionals interested in their own performance, something stopped working...What happened? Professionals began to feel uncomfortable. They felt threatened by the thought of having their own role in the organization examined with a critical eye. Thus, because they felt that they were well paid (and considered their employees to be, for the most part, devoted and honest), the idea that their performance was perhaps not the best gave them a sense of guilt' (Argyris, 1991).
18. Going back to a discussion in Crozier (1995).

2 The Customer's Victory

To understand what is meant here by the 'customer's victory', we will have to go back to the debate over globalization first mentioned in the introduction. As we saw, the idea of globalization today is no longer contested, but this is not to say that the concept is accepted everywhere in the same way, or that its consequences do not undergo harsh criticism. In many countries, we find two schools of thought. On one hand, there is the school which, although having observed the inevitableness of globalization, does not take for granted the elimination of nation-states.[1] Instead, a strong state should increasingly regulate the effects of globalization and protect its citizens from the more serious consequences. This would mean voluntarily bowing out, 'politically', from the hyper-financialization of the world. This line of thinking is the exact opposite of the one proclaimed on billboards in the United States, such as the well-known slogan 'Government is the problem, free enterprise is the solution'. On the other hand, there is the school, in the minority, that suggests that we might, by cutting ourselves off from the rest of the world and refocusing our energies on national culture, tradition, morality and so on, escape the generalized movement towards a global economy.

These are not very realistic. Robert Reich[2] clearly defined globalization and its consequences on a country, by adopting a distinction between American society and the American economy:

> We are experiencing a transformation which will reorganize politics and the economy in the next century. There will be no national products or national technologies, no national businesses or industries. National economies will no longer exist, at least in the way in which we conceive of them today. All that will remain rooted within borders are the people who make up a nation...the underlying question concerns the future of American society as distinct from the American economy, and the destiny of the majority of Americans, who are losers in global competition.

The idea of a dual society returns, with on one hand those who can participate in globalization, benefit from it and free themselves once and

for all from the former local dependencies which have left a deep historical imprint,[3] and then those who are subject to its consequences, with few
means to react and intervene in their own fate.

This winner/loser vision is not wrong, at least in the short run, which
is, after all, as far as we can see in respect of the phenomenon of globalization. But what is of interest is that this vision can be found in the workplace and in organizations, starting with what seems to be one of the most
immediate and abrupt consequences of globalization: the customer's
victory. This is not a new observation, no more than the intuition that this
victory must have irreversible consequences for organizations which
produce goods and services. It was at the root of the re-engineering
process, which many countries, including France, rejected categorically[4]
without reflecting more fully on the extent of the preconceived notions
from which this movement stems, looking only at the technical aspects,
most often only to refute them. 'Economic power has been handed over
from the producer to the consumer…mass production, more quality, more
for the money, more choice, more service', write Hammer and Champy.[5]
This is about as clear as one can get concerning the consequences of such
a movement.

From an entirely different perspective, and with quite different conclusions, Sami Naïr says much the same thing:[6]

> In its 'chemically pure' form, the legitimization of liberal globalization hinges
> on praising the consumer as king. Since the market constitutes the most effec-
> tive mechanism for distributing wealth, and since globalization is now helping
> to tear down all borders – be they geographical, cultural, of the nation or the
> state–borders which, up till now, have held it back from fulfilling its universal
> vocation, globalization must now be allowed to run its full course. For the final
> result will be the victory of the consumer… If the latter is not the 'end of
> history', it is at least the 'direction of history'.

Rifkin offers yet a third version of this observation:

> The 'personalized' consumer is now starting to displace 'standardized' distribu-
> tion amid the various forms of competition in which businesses engage in the
> hopes of winning customers over, one by one, while at the same time attempt-
> ing to keep costs associated with maintaining a stockpile of products as low as
> possible.'[7]

This is thus the same vision, today commonplace in many companies,
built around 'disinterested consensus' which keeps us from understanding
the actual consequences in day-to-day life in the workplace. In their heated
battle to hold at bay the drastic changes which are on their way, bureau-

crats – a term which we will define more precisely in the next chapter – 'swallow' the idea of the customer's victory, but see it as little more than a tasteless pill. The idea must thus be explored more seriously in three directions. First, what does it mean that the 'customer has won' in daily life, but conceptually as well, in terms of the distribution of power? Next, if the customer has truly won, and must be listened to at all costs, then how do organizations react to this new constraint? Finally, why does this victory present a fundamental problem of the organization, as defined in the preceding sections?

From a scarce product to a scarce customer

To more fully comprehend what the customer's victory means in concrete, day-to-day terms, let us take a simple example with which the author has had first-hand experience. The example concerns a medium-size town (of about 20 000 residents) located some 50 kilometres from Paris. Thirty years ago, there were about as many people. But in those days prospective car buyers in the town had only one vendor to turn to, in this case a Renault dealership. When asked about the availability of an automobile, the dealer would explain that it was a difficult time to place an order, and after consulting his books and calling the manufacturer, would say that with a little luck a vehicle could be brought in within two or three months, provided that the buyer was not too set on a particular colour or horsepower. The customer, delighted by such good fortune, would have celebrated the event that very evening with friends and family. Along the same lines, some readers might recall how difficult it was to come by tyres, even well after the end of World War II.

Today, in the very same town, there are 13 automobile dealerships, each one fighting for a piece of the local market through aggressive advertising campaigns. Prospective buyers, off to test drive a few models in the early afternoon, could easily be on their way home two to three hours later in a new car, the details of insurance and temporary registration all worked out, credit established in no more than 15 minutes, and a substantial reduction off the base price thrown into the bargain.

This is the revolution. We are moving from a long-standing period in which what was scarce was the product, to a period where what is scarce is the customer. This then is what is happening, the scarcity relationship is being overturned, with far-reaching consequences. When the product was rare, it was costly, a classic economic observation. In fact, this costliness involved three dimensions: the price, of course; the quality, in the most basic sense of the term, that of the product; but also in terms of quality in a more complex sense, that is, the quality of the way the goods or service are produced and delivered to the customer. Here then is what we are interested in, 'organizational costliness', for it leads to a first observation, which we will develop fully in the following chapter: 'organizational cost-liness' is the cost which a producer, in a superior position, requires that customers pay, permitting it, the producer, to maintain modes of func-tioning based on its own strategies, its own human or technical constraints. When, on the other hand, the customer wins out and the scarcity relationship is reversed, power in the relationship is also reversed, and not just economic power as suggested by Hammer and Champy. Power pure and simple, or global power, if you will.

Although the observation that power passes from the hands of the producer to those of the customer is true, it is not very specific. Customer's victory, yes. Victory over the producer, indeed, but actually over the producer's process (the way in which a product is made and offered) and all that is tied to it in terms of the management of individuals (schedules, guarantees, status) which bears a price, once again not only monetary but also in terms of customer 'convenience'. Later on, as we consider the nature of a bureaucracy in more detail, we will be able to grasp more fully the after-effects of this veritable earthquake.

The hazards of segmentation

It is worth mentioning here that some organizations actually weaken the notion of the customer's victory, especially those for which this victory bears the most severe consequences. These organizations react by develop-ing, on one hand, a new function, a kind of 'listening management programme', one more vertical structure; and on the other, yet more sophisticated traditional marketing tools, so as to keep tabs on the market. These reactions make it possible to work with 'virtual customers', customers who can be made to say just about anything through the manip-ulation of statistics, and who therefore place few real constraints on busi-ness since they do not really exist. The religion of numbers, of quantities and statistics, of 'segmentation', is moreover the target of growing criti-cism from all sides. Some point out the chronic inability of quantitative knowledge to comprehend the subtlety of consumers, their real satisfaction and expectations, *a fortiori* their customs, even the complex evolution of their way of life and standard of living.[8] Others viciously condemn the idea of tampering with numbers and the dehumanized nature of the entire process.[9] Beyond the rather emotional arguments, Edgar Morin makes it clear that quantitative analysis takes the place of reality, ensuring the survival of bureaucracy: '...there is a depoliticization of politics, which self-destruct within administrative structures, technical considerations (expertise), the economy, and quantification (polls and statistics)'.[10]

Numbers set us all the more ill at ease as we realize that there is little real connection between the sophistication of the tools of analysis which are used to probe the customers, and the ability of the organization to satisfy them and gain their loyalty. We can even observe today that 'market segmentation', an expression which can be taken literally, has led to a re-segmentation of organizations, built around categories of customers. This has developed just as rigidly as when segmentation was based on tasks, one after another. Since customers now belong to a category – a category that is of course too strict to be able to take into account customer complexity – they are presumed to be satisfied, all because the organization has provided that category with a special division. It is trying to solve the problem by simply reworking the 'structural puzzle', as we already pointed out, except that the real problem has not been addressed.

How not to listen

To take this a bit further, let us turn to a simple example, which we will then develop with a slightly more complicated case study.

Take for example a European telecommunications firm which, just like its sister companies, will be facing deregulation in the near future. This company grew out of the long-standing management traditions of the public sector. Agent loyalty is not a problem, their status is secure, and clearly defines their rights and obligations, as well as how their careers can evolve, and how they are to be remunerated. These rights are linked to seniority, and not to the business activity of the company. Recall that monopolistic situations have been particularly favourable to the development of these advantages, the cost of which has been externalized on to the customer – the user – who at the time could do nothing about it.

In order to match the growing competition, our company has developed remarkable marketing skills, and has conducted an impressive number of customer profile studies. Similarly, it has developed elaborate methods of measuring customer satisfaction, which it does on a regular basis. The surprising fact is that, despite the quality of the company's products, which are as good as any, its customers, especially those who generate the greatest amount of business, seem ready to take any chance they can get to head over to the competition. In its attempt to deal with this paradox, the company has tried offering more and more products and services, targeting the categories of customers which it has identified, but seems all the less able to keep customers from taking their business elswhere.

To better understand this situation, let us take a look at one of the company's customers, John Doe, a 'professional', according to the company's own system of classification. The company, having identified specific needs for this particular segment of the market, has provided Mr Doe with special agencies. He was informed by mail that 'his' agency had opened (the possessive was used so as to create a sense of intimacy), which he rightaway decided to call up in order to have a fax line installed in his home. John is told by a company representative, obviously well-trained in 'the customer welcome process', that the company regrets that it cannot accept orders over the phone. Surprised by the lack of confidence in the very medium which, after all, the company is promoting, he asks how then he should place an order. He is informed that orders must be placed by mail – and cannot help but wonder whether this company is simply trying to generate some business for former co-workers at the postal service.[11]

In any case, 10 days after mailing his letter, our 'professional' receives a highly personalized reply bearing the name and address of a 'correspondent' on the letterhead. The letter states that the new phone line will be installed that very day, within a window of about two hours, so as to avoid any unnecessary delay. Suddenly faced with the prospect of having to stay home from work (Mr Doe is after all a 'professional'), he picks up the phone and asks to speak to his new correspondent. The representative on the line is surprised by his request, and informs him that the title 'correspondent' simply refers to the person who entered his file into the computer database. After being transferred to another representative, he explains that he cannot possibly wait at home for the fax line to be installed. The representative is sorry about the mix-up, adding that the company could not foresee that he would be away. Surprised that they could not have simply called to set up an appointment, he is told that of course they had tried to contact him, but that since he was not at home (he is of course a professional) a time had been set anyway and the letter sent out. At the suggestion that a message could have been left on his answering machine, the employee, who incidentally pays no attention to the customer's remark that the answering machine had been purchased through the very same agency, states that the company does not conduct business in that fashion. Finally, at the 'professional's' suggestion that they call in the evening, the representative retorts that the company has not yet resorted to working after hours.

What is going on here? The organization has in fact addressed the wrong problem, or, at the very least, has not understood the scope of the problem. Increasingly forced to listen to its customers, the company first reacts by offering more products. In this respect, which is moreover how the company determines whether or not its customers are satisfied, the company is doing an outstanding job. But, as we will see later on, the product, as a function of demand (its technical characteristics), is decreasingly what differentiates competitors. Competing products are increasingly similar, regardless of their apparent sophistication.[12] The 'differential advantage' then, resides more in the way the product is produced and/or the way it is offered. That is to say, in the organization, the one which develops products, the one which manufactures products, and the one which offers them, and in the ability of these three to co-operate.

In the case of this company, the products are technically very good and their price very reasonable. However, the organization which offers them has in no way 'listened' to the customer. It is simply entrapped in its own norms and procedures, in the way it develops its database, in the routine and red tape which are part and parcel of the way it manages public relations and work schedules. Suddenly, the professional customer has disappeared. And the reason he is gone is that the complexity of his needs were not understood. The company never dealt concretely with his daily life, including when he goes to work, when he stays home, how his phone is used by his family during the day and for work purposes at night. He was no more than a *virtual* professional, around which no concrete organization had been set up either for him, or for the other members of the organization, nor had a pricing policy been established which could take into account how he really uses the telephone.

All that had been set up was a means of sidestepping the issue, a screen, a decoy – the words are not too strong – which simply stand in as the symbols of listening, but they are not listening.[13] By dealing with listening as a function – an aspect of marketing in this case – the organization spares itself from taking a good hard look at itself, that is, more directly, at how appropriate its own modes of functioning are for the customer which it intends to serve. This is exactly what it needed to see. Listening to the customer, which has become so necessary, so inevitable now that the customer stands as the winner, confronts bureaucracies with very difficult and disturbing problems. Listening simply cannot be reduced to yet another function – bureaucracies excel at that – no more than quality could be reduced to a function in the 1980s, despite many attempts to do so.

Much more than a function, it is a mode of functioning, organization as defined in Chapter 1. Listening is a set of behaviours, of arrangements, of co-operative efforts; it includes how employees' careers evolve, and through this their status in the company, their benefits, their privileges. In order to truly listen to the customer, one must begin by taking a closer look at all of these various domains. In many cases, listening can be quite painful.

The case of a British catering company

The case of a British catering company provides a good illustration of what is meant by listening. The company in question is a world leader in its domain which includes providing food service in various institutions: schools, businesses and offices. Its structure is simple: the country is divided into regions, each of which is headed by a regional director, assisted by a small team which is responsible for human resources, marketing support of base-level units, and the development of quality control strategies. In turn, each region is divided into sectors, which are under the direction of sector supervisors, who are generally young graduates of business schools, and who themselves put pressure on the restaurant managers, who are responsible for the day-to-day production and delivery of meals. Note that a considerable part of the salary of the regional heads is variable, their bonuses related to two criteria: on one hand, the profits achieved within their region; on the other, the number of meals served, so that the top of the line (restaurants and business clubs, for example) will not be overdeveloped to the detriment of restaurants with low profit margins. The variable portion of the sector supervisors' salaries is calculated in the same way, but represents a considerably smaller part of their total earnings. Lastly, the manager is paid a fixed salary, which increases with seniority and according to the relative clout of restaurant for which he or she is responsible. Finally, we should point out that the regional director appoints the sector supervisors in the different regions, knowing that some of them have better reputations than others in terms of their profitability or 'risk', which boils down to customer loyalty.

As we focus on the day-to-day activities of this organization, we find several interesting facts:

■ Relations between the regional directors and their sector supervisors are courteous and convivial, although it is fairly rare for them to meet given the expanse of each region. Overall, communication between these levels is fairly superficial. There is quite a bit of talk, but not much is said: there is often more discussion about world events than about work.

■ Sector supervisors themselves have few occasions to get together. Their territories cover a lot of ground and they are responsible for a large number of restaurants. When they do meet up, once again we see conviviality; food is often served for example, and once again work is not the major topic of discussion.

■ Sector supervisors and managers seem to be subject to very intense pressure. The former are constantly complaining about this, to the extent that company directors are concerned, and talk seriously about tackling the problem, although they do not have a clue how to go about it. Restaurant managers also suffer from pressure, but are less willing to discuss it openly.

The reason is that they are the scapegoats within this organization: the regional director and sector supervisors agree that managers are not very competent and are therefore generally unable to take an objective view of the situation. Management laments having to fire a certain number of them on a regular basis.

■ In last place, there are the customers: those who, it is important to note, sign the contracts and not those who eat at the restaurants (whom we might call the guests). The customers express great satisfaction. They feel that the company, and more specifically the sector supervisors who are their real contacts, take good care of them, listen closely to their problems, and seem always to do their utmost to satisfy them. The customers and sector supervisors meet moreover outside of the workplace, in gatherings organized by the latter. The regional director, who deals only with several of the more significant clients, is not associated with these events. Finally, the customers share the negative opinion of the restaurant managers, whom they consider to be the weak link in the chain of this organization.

Satisfied customers, people who have been 'listened to': what differences are there between this and the case of the telecommunications company which might explain these relationships? Certainly not the people involved and their loyalty, but the organization itself. Let us try to understand how it functions: all the young sector supervisors express a desire for autonomy, freedom to organize their work and their 'rounds' just as they see fit. They work within a large region, which they know well, and are in contact with customers whose concerns they have identified, and which they try to address. Any intervention into their operations by the regional director is viewed negatively, even as a kind of sanction. In any case, the directors neither have the time nor the training to keep a close eye on the supervisors. They leave them a great deal of freedom (autonomy) so long as everything runs smoothly. What might be a 'problem' for this organization? Most certainly the loss of a customer, which can easily happen in this very competitive environment, and which translates into a rapid drop in the number of meals served, thereby affecting the regional director's bonus. A decrease in profitability as well, which has the same effect. So, by reconstructing the triangle of the regional director, the sector supervisor and the customer, we have a good model of how the organization operates: the regional director yields full autonomy to the sector supervisor, according to the latter's own wishes, so long as the two criteria on which the director is evaluated and paid are not jeopardized. Should this happen, the director intervenes immediately; to avoid such a scenario and remain autonomous, the sector supervisor almost literally 'hangs on to' the customers, attempting to anticipate their needs and satisfy them. This is the classic model of an organization operating within a highly competitive market, in which armed peace between the travelling sector supervisors and the sedentary regional director works to the advantage of a customer who holds the key to the relationship: the contract.

The limitations of this mode of functioning are of course easy to identify. It is based entirely on the fact that one of the participants pays the price: the restaurant manager must work out the agreement struck between the sector supervisor and the customer, the conditions of which almost always border on the impossible. From a certain point of view, restaurant managers 'pay for' the sector supervisors' freedom, and whenever the latter complain about being under pressure, whether they know it or not, they actually transfer most of this pressure over to the restaurant managers. It is thus a system which carries a heavy human cost – this is the cost of the customer's victory, a point which we intend to get back to later on – a system which every day wastes a great deal of know-how, focused on the short term, much more reactive than proactive. But let us consider it first and foremost as a reaction to the advantage now held by the customer, a reaction involving constraints, in a sense. The system is not very sophisticated, implying a physical environment in which work is hard and uncomfortable. But after all, since when does a customer worry about the well-being of a company?

Getting out of the beaten tracks

Other businesses have found more elaborate ways of listening to their customers, but in each case they proceed in terms of their own mode of functioning, and not in terms of a function. Richard Normann and Rafaël

Ramirez have outlined the path chosen by Ikea[14] which consists in getting the customer to help co-produce real value. They summarize what they consider to be the strategy of the future as follows:

> Companies do not only create value by making more intelligent product offers, but by developing more intelligent relationships with their customers and suppliers. To do this, the businesses must continuously reevaluate and redefine their abilities and their relationships so as to maintain the flexibility of these value-creating systems, keeping them new and reactive. In this new value strategy the on-going dialogue between the company and its customers can explain the success and the survival of certain businesses, and the decline and failure of others.[15]

It is interesting to consider L'Oréal's answer to the problem, which is beyond doubt one of the most original, since it is so far removed from traditional management models. In this high-performance corporation, strategy is the number one 'intangible asset'. To put it briefly, within the organization there is no internal monopoly. By this we mean that in its primary domains – those of marketing and commercial activity – no one decides anything all alone, and more importantly, knowing just who should decide what is never perfectly clear. The launching of a product for example, involves the director of international marketing, the director of marketing of the brand name under which the product is to be sold, the director of marketing of the country in which the product will be tested, and so on all at once. Everything must be negotiated, each participant must 'confront' the others, using the in-house expression. In this confrontation, one's position within the hierarchy matters very little. This is no doubt why there is no organizational chart, and why no one has even bothered to create one. The decisive factor in a confrontation – and one must know how to win a confrontation in order to make a career within the organization – is the knowledge of a given market which one can contribute to the negotiation. This knowledge carries with it personal involvement in the outcome and is thus a constraint, but it is at the same time the argument which causes others to give in. The loose structure of the organization – the exact opposite of a bureaucracy as we will see in the following chapter – is not a sign of disorganization, as some of the American executives in the corporation seem to fear. It is really a kind of 'political' system, in which the market is the players' principal resource. Once again, but in ways that are quite different from those of Ikea, the border between the company and its market fade away, beyond theoretical organizational charts. This being the case, in order to function in this way, several conditions must be met. It is worth stating these here if only to temper some of the enthusiasm of those who wish to follow the example.

First, a system of sanctions must exist to put the dream that everyone has 'the right to make a mistake' back into proper perspective. In a system which snaps its fingers at hierarchical structures, the need for a code of ethics is obvious. By code of ethics understand a set of unwritten rules – a culture, some might say – which limits the unpredictability of the participants' behaviour. This means making any dishonesty in negotiation, in regard to the market and its possibilities for example, very costly. Participants must rely on real knowledge, which is why there is personal commitment. Otherwise, there would be 'no holds barred', which is not the case in this company. Over time, the lack of a code of ethics would break the organization apart and lead it to ruin.

Similarly there must be some kind of arbitration, generally seated at the highest level. This guarantees that a decision can be made carefully, within reasonable time limits, and at the same time encourages the local actors to make the decision themselves: indeed, recourse to a third party, as in any organization, implies a price to be paid, in this case objectives which are generally more difficult than those which the actors would have settled upon themselves.

So as to keep the human cost of this kind of operation within reason, and it is high, there must be a human resources strategy which is flexible and individualized, able to move individuals about, taking them off the battleground when they are worn out, giving them a chance to recover. The strategy must compensate employees in a way that is fully linked to their success in the markets and business activity for which they are responsible even early on in their career.

Finally, within this arrangement, production can in no way dictate its own constraints. Not that production is of no importance: on the contrary, a great deal of energy is invested in production; not that quality is not as good here as elsewhere: the company could not survive under such conditions. But in the context of overall functioning, production is secondary to the business as a whole, akin to what technology was for President Kennedy when he declared that America would send a man to the moon well ahead of the nation's technical ability to do so, or what day-to-day operations were to General Charles de Gaulle, when he declared that they must keep up with the will of the nation.

Human resources management, as a necessary counterpart to the customer's victory

Taking a few steps back now, what have we learned from this first look at the consequences of the customer's victory for organizations? First and foremost that an appeal is being made to the organization itself and not just a few of its members (the marketing division or the front office). It is not enough to send a few good soldiers off to the front lines to face head on the ever-increasing demands of customers. Bravery and loyalty are quickly spent if the organization does not follow, or if the soldier deserts to join the army of consumers: this is a classic mechanism, which has been with us for some time now.[16] Whenever members of an organization are in contact with the environment, and the organization does not allow them to satisfy that environment, they then become its representatives, its lobbyists at the heart of their own company or administrative structure, which they will then criticize even more vehemently than the customers themselves, proving in this way how flexible they are faced with a sclerotic bureaucratic body, insensitive as it is to the expectations of the general public. In this relationship, these members 'sell' themselves against their own organization. For a long time it was believed that this model worked only for administrative structures, especially those in France, but today, in fact, we see that it is spreading as a result of the pressure which customers are exerting on organizations in the competitive sector, organizations which do not understand what it is they are being asked to do. In the following chapters, we will re-encounter this problem in the air transportation industry, as well as in banking and insurance.

Furthermore, organizations differ in the way in which they manage problems, for they are not all equal in their ability to confront them. This observation is central to this book. However they might deal with these problems, we might add, there is always a human cost which companies are more or less able to reabsorb. Although we have yet to discuss the profound nature of this cost, its presence is a sure sign that the worlds which are being rebuilt around the customers, attempting to meet their needs, are *de facto* more uncomfortable than those which were in place when customers were of relatively little concern, or when solutions were sought in ways other than a major organizational change. This is not a disinterested observation: it brings up the issue of opposition to change, not as a psychological problem – that would be a natural, 'cultural' tendency of individuals to resist change – but as a practical and very concrete behaviour, calculated in terms of the cost/advantage relationship. The 'less' we are involved, at least in the transitional phase which we see today, is also a 'less' in terms of advantages, comfort and possibilities to live in a world where there is much pressure.

When this idea is taken a little further – less comfort in the most general sense of the term – we begin to see just how important the management of human resources is in an organization's struggle to adapt to the customer's victory. First, since the environment is increasingly hostile, if the company does not want to settle for 'squeezing the lemon' and then throwing out the rind, it must manage careers as a function of this new deal. If not, the human cost becomes quite considerable, and even if the cynicism of those involved – and we know how corrosive that can be for organizations – allows them to accept this human cost, it will in time have serious repercussions on the business itself, whose members experience the company exclusively in a utilitarian mode. There are many today who are quick to point out the dangers of such a relationship: Robert H. Waterman's advice to 'put your people first', is by no means at odds with customer satisfaction, it is rather one of the conditions for it.[17] This is echoed by the words of a particular human resource director, who, at a meeting with his company's board of divisional directors, compared the work environment to a sporting event between professional athletes under constant pressure, who must, by definition, be even better during an actual event than in training. One participant in this meeting asked the human resource director for how long one might expect to remain a top-level athlete, and what one would be expected to do later on in the company.

The second major aspect of human resource management concerns the criteria for the management of individuals – how they are evaluated, promoted, remunerated and so on. These become, as in the case of the British catering company, keys to behaviour modification, and it is always surprising to note just how many businesses have still not bridged the gap between their overall corporate strategy in the matter, and their ability to generate business and serve their customers. Make no mistake: this is not meant as a throwback to the old Taylorian observation that individuals at work are motivated exclusively by monetary concerns. There are many other things which can be offered to make the new constraints more acceptable. The catering company was a good illustration that the actors' autonomy, when properly regulated by the organization – here by profitability and the number of meals served – can be a powerful lever in getting the company to meet the needs of the customer. One might object that it is precisely this quest for unbridled autonomy which keeps public bureaucracies from learning anything new. This is true, but those bureaucracies are characterized by a large gap between how careers, salaries and so on are administered on one hand, and the business outcome on the other. Hence there is no compensation for autonomy here. It is not a constructive term of exchange at the heart of the leader–customer representative–customer trilogy.[18] We have finally begun to glimpse the problem of the 'fuzziness' of certain organizations, an aspect which it is not worth contrasting with clarity, in which there seems to be no special virtue, but instead with monopolies.

This explains our hesitation to follow the pundits of re-engineering in their passion for processes. Of course, on careful reading, they themselves reveal this hesitation. Hammer and Champy write: 'The fourth key word in our definition – of re-engineering – is "process". It is also the most important word, the one which presents the most serious problems for executives... An operational process is a series of activities which, based on one or several entries (inputs), produces a result (output) representing some value for the customer.'[19] Two hundred pages later, the authors back off from this, enumerating the errors which lie in wait for a re-engineering program: '[one of the errors] is to look only at the processes, to not take into account the new systems of evaluation, the redefinition of hierarchical powers, the transformation of the relationships among personnel.'[20] In fact, behind processes, even with the slightly different meaning offered here, there is co-operation between the actors, which escapes precise definition, which is an unstable equilibrium, a policy within the organization itself. Co-operation cannot be decreed, nor can it be codified into a set of rules and procedures which would form 'the layman's guide to the appropriate method of co-operation between members of the association'.

Conversely, it assumes that once a favourable environment has been created (through personnel management, or exchanges in autonomy, for example), the organization will agree to go no further in defining itself, nor even in attempting to understand its own mechanisms. Now we understand why these fuzzy organizations very rarely accept that their 'culture' should be rendered explicit. They fear the reification of that which must remain implicit. And they know just what they are doing.

Notes

1. For example, Ohmae (1996).
2. Reich (1992), pp. 3–9.
3. Cf. Castel (1995).
4. Michel Drancourt for example writes: 'A lot of fun has been poked in France at the re-engineering movement from which we have only retained the "nuts and bolts". We did not understand that it was a management and business organization revolution, directed no longer just at the huge American market, but at the conquest of global markets as well' (Drancourt, 1997, p. 33).

5. Hammer and Champy (1993), p. 27.
6. Morin and Naïr (1997), p. 4.
7. Rifkin (1996), p. 150.
8. Uchitelle (1997).
9. Viviane Forrester writes: 'We can truly count on a good deal of cheerful deception, such as the one which eliminated between 250 000 and 300 000 unemployed workers from the statistics in a single blow…by striking from the lists those who do at least 78 hours of work per month, in other words, less than two weeks, and without any benefits. It was a solution waiting to be found! Bear in mind the unchanged fate of bodies and souls hidden behind the statistics, of little importance as compared to how a particular calculation is carried out. Numbers are what count, even if they reflect no real value, nothing organic, no result, even if they only signify deception' (Forrester, 1996, pp. 12–13).
10. Morin and Naïr (1997), p. 21.
11. In this country, national telecommunications and the postal service operated formerly as one unit.
12. For more definitive proof, consider investment banking products and related services, each one more immaterial than the last, each one more complex, but never really any different.
13. What is being challenged here is not the goodwill of individuals, nor some intentionally manipulatory endeavour on the part of the organization. The problem is the mode of reasoning employed.
14. Ikea is a Swedish firm which specializes in furniture and other decorative products for the home. The company markets some of its products by manufacturing them according to customer specifications. Customers come into the store, choose the model they would like, its colour, the materials to be used and so on, and only then is the item manufactured and delivered.
15. Normann and Ramirez (1993), pp. 65–75.
16. Gremion (1976).
17. Waterman (1995); see, for example, Ch. 5, 'People first at Federal Express', pp. 87–110.
18. See the analysis presented in Dupuy (1990), **8**(2): 4–12.
19. Hammer and Champy (1993), p. 45.
20. *Ibid.*, p. 227.

3
What is a Bureaucracy?

To take an interest in bureaucracy is not to look back at the past, but towards the future. The central hypothesis of this book is that the end of bureaucracies, as they will be defined in a few moments, is the number one hell to face in the transformation of companies and organizations in coming years. It is no secret: there is not one management textbook or analysis of world trends that is not keenly interested in the end of bureaucracies, regardless of the author's point of view: 'Today in the realm of organizations we see and suffer from cumbersome bureaucracies which, more than ever, are signs of the poor management of meaning.'[1] To which Waterman adds a more precise definition: 'The problem is as follows: the bureaucracy, our most traditional form of organization, was created to manage the day-to-day problems of organizations: the sales department sells, manufacturing manufactures, and so on. So long as economic activity does not change too quickly, bureaucracies get along fairly well. But things are changing quickly.'[2] So why has this disjointed, compartmentalized mode of functioning taken the upper hand over other forms of organization? Robert Reich explains it as follows,[3] based on the American situation:

> American bureaucratic companies were organized around the model of military bureaucracies for the efficient deployment of plans developed well in advance. It is perhaps not by chance that war veterans who entered the major American companies in the 1950s very naturally re-created at the centre of these companies the military model of a bureaucracy. They were set up along the lines of a military hierarchy, with chains of command, control methods, rank, divisions with division leaders, and procedures outlining the decision-making process. If you have a question, check the manual!

After presenting Reich's thesis, Rifkin adds: 'The managerial system of business organization is a giant oaf, a powerful producer capable of creating sizable quantities of standardized commodities, but lacking the flexibility to make nimble adjustments so as to adapt to rapid fluctuations in domestic or global markets.'[4]

The story of an evolution

One key idea stands out in these quotations: the bureaucratic form of organization belonged to a moment in history during which products (either goods or services) were scarce. In this sense, a bureaucracy is intimately linked to mass production and, no doubt, to a democratic way of thinking. It corresponds to the arrival of a new age in the evolution of humankind: in economic terms, by making available to the greatest number the goods and services to which they may legitimately aspire; and in politics, by setting up a state of human rights which presupposes rules and procedures and their application. This is why for Max Weber,[5] as well as for Henri Mintzberg,[6] bureaucracy designates a collective order, a legitimate state of domination based upon a set of rules and procedures, a professional and process-based organization. From this perspective, one could define the bureaucracy as an organization whose responsibility it is to produce both general and impersonal rules and to apply them. Furthermore, this 'mode' of doing things must apply as much to the people the bureaucracy serves as to its own members. This is the opposite of the 'organic' mode, that of the artisan class as defined by Burns and Stalker.[7] It can similarly be found in the works of Henri Fayol.[8] Virtuous towards its subjects, bureaucracy in this paradigm would also be good to its members, ensuring equality for all in law, acting as the *de facto* guarantor of civil rights, whether it be with respect to a political state (rights of the citizen), or an economic state (rights of the customer).

Yet as time passed, doubt began to cast a shadow over virtuous bureaucracy. Although some authors were able to demonstrate how these organizations have a tremendous ability to adapt from day to day, in particular by betraying their 'Weberian' mission to apply rules and procedures,[9] it has become increasingly clear that the bureaucratic way of doing things primarily serves internal concerns related to the protection of the organizations' members, rather than the establishment of a form of government working on behalf of everyone's happiness. Or at least that is how bureaucrats have evolved! Michel Crozier was the first, and, in the author's opinion, in a quite definite manner, to identify the key characteristics of a modern bureaucratic organization[10] as it existed in the 1960s – centralization, stratification and its method of human resource management – by bringing to the fore systemic aspects as opposed to an individualized view of the 'bureaucrat'. He described centralization in a way which still today makes leaders of large international corporations jump because it comes so close to what they observe but dare not admit. Centralization results from an imbalance between the centre which is supposed to decide everything although it is caught up in endless petty decisions and lacks the information to do so, and an outer sphere which is all the more free and uncontrolled as a result of having to apply the inapplicable rules established by the under-informed centre. The author does not share Michel Crozier's view that 'The Bureaucratic Phenomenon' owes its success in the United States to the fact that it helped explain French bureaucracy; it simply helped explain the American businesses whose functioning is described by Robert Reich.[11] Similarly, he identified in a decisive manner 'the fear of face-to-face interaction', which for our purposes we will reinterpret in terms of non-co-operation, as well as the gap between what employees do and how personnel are managed.

Taylor, or the sole rationality

From the standpoint of this book, we have to go one step further and shed light on an analysis of bureaucracy which is less endogenous and which can reveal effects on the environment, which we denote here by the generic term 'customers'. To do this, we must go back to the idea mentioned earlier of the customer's victory over the producer, its process and its human resource constraints. With this in mind, I would like to propose the following definition for a bureaucracy:

> A bureaucracy is an organization which translates its technical constraints (the task), its human constraints (personnel), or both, spontaneously and systematically into its mode of functioning (that is to say, without wondering whether there are other alternatives).

This definition is valid for industry as well as the service sector, for both companies and public administration. It underscores that the most fundamental trait of a bureaucracy is that the criteria upon which its organization is based are endogenous and considered to be universal, unavoidable and unquestionable. This definition will allow us to begin where Taylor[12] left off and work our way up to the customer's victory.

It was indeed Taylor who proposed that an organization can be built around technical tasks, underscoring the universal nature of this kind of organization.[13] Jeremy Rifkin[14] summarizes Taylor's principle as follows:

> With the help of a chronometer, Taylor reduced the different tasks of workers to their smallest identifiable operational parts, then measured the latter to obtain the minimum amount of time required for a given task under optimal operating conditions. His research permitted calibrating worker performance to

within almost a fraction of a second. By calculating the average and optimal lengths of each part of workers' tasks, Taylor was able to make recommendations on the most minute details of the execution of tasks, so as to save precious seconds, even fractions of a second.

Each and every word is important in this reading of the logic of time and movement, but clearly the one word which appears most frequently as the base unit of scientific management is 'task'. Let us stop here a moment, and make a rather simple observation: we are not asking whether an organization set up around tasks is possible or even desirable, it is simply what we observe. This kind of organization represented a significant step forward, and has been thoroughly discussed in the literature. It made possible both mass production and lower product cost, thereby making products available to the greatest number. It likewise made possible 'mass management', one of the conditions of Weberian democracy; it was even a source of inspiration to the founders of total quality approaches, such as Taïchi Ono. But to conclude from all this that it is the only possible form of organization would be a serious mistake, a fact made clear by the customer's victory. Taylorian thinking, then as now, makes the same mistake. It jumps from a hypothetical phase – organization around tasks is the best way of assuring mass production whenever the product is scarce – to a universal proposition: it is the only possible way (an approach in terms of 'one best way').

This mode of reasoning which is built not only around the primacy of technical constraints but also around the idea that there is one and only one way of running an organization, is still today the dominant model, probably because we are aware of so few alternatives. Once this model has been accepted, we lose the ability to distance ourselves from technical constraints, and require others to suffer the consequences. Why? Because the responsibility lies not with us, which would be clearly self-serving, but with science, which is above special interests. By claiming that the primacy of the producer is scientifically based, we can set up such unquestionable organizations that to dispute them would be nothing short of revolutionary. But what can lead to such a revolution, or, in other words, how and for whom is such reasoning a problem?

The professor, his cards and the bureaucracy

So long as the customers have no say in the matter, since they are the 'losers', they agree to give in to the whole set of bureaucratic constraints. A 'set' because the loose thread which appeared with the task has been pulled and the bureaucratic bobbin has come unwound: tasks lead us to procedures, procedures to geographic separation, separation to schedules, schedules to job status: and thus, step by step, we begin to see just how big the monster really is. The customer who has to give in to the producer is also the one who has to send his or her child to a given state school, the one who has to run to the local retailer not when there is a pressing need, but when the store is open. This is the customer who has to follow a complex process of rules and procedures, running from one place to the next, all because the system was not designed for the customer's convenience, but for the bureaucrats who have certain tasks to do, while other tasks which are not part of their job responsibilities are not accomplished. The key symbolic word in the Kafkaesque world of bureaucracies might well be 'file': 'I have your file', 'Where is your file?', 'Do I have a good file?', 'Your file is incomplete', 'Your file was not sent over to me', and so on.

Let us turn to a simple illustration. When visiting professors arrive in a state university in the United States, right off the bat they need to get hold of two important 'tools': a bank card and a university identity card (which provides access to various campus services). The two cards look alike: they are about the same size and shape, have a magnetic strip with a picture and signature of the holder printed on the back and an identification number of about the same number of digits on both cards. How are they obtained? For the bank card, it takes about 10 minutes at the bank, during which time different accounts are opened. The bank employee offers the bank card, suggests getting a picture ID, snaps the picture in a little room set up just for this purpose, and delivers the card. In a short span of time, one person carries out a set of tasks revolving around the customer. This is a case of 'seamless service', as we will see later on. The employee is friendly and courteous, but more importantly, we see that the organization is itself built around the customer, and to do this, the very job description of bank employees was redefined and enlarged: they must be photographers, printers, and of course able to open accounts!

As for the university card, the courtesy or dedication of employees, their obvious desire to be of service are not a problem here either. But the intent of the organization is another matter altogether! After a visit to the Office of International Services, seekers of an identity card have to run over to a health insurance agency to pick up several important papers before returning to the first office. They must then return to their own department, where they might find out that it will take several days for the necessary paperwork to be approved by the dean and the department head. When all of the paperwork is in order, the journey ends at a final stop with the photographer, who asks new faculty members to stop by a week later to pick up the magic card.

The first organization is built around the customer, the second around the tasks and their segmentation. The first offers one location, the second several journeys from one specialized office to the next. Given a choice, we can easily imagine that a customer would prefer providers, public or private, to reorganize around customers and their way of thinking, which is by definition very different from that of the bureaucracy. This calls into question not only the 'organization' in the largest sense of the term, including here what employees actually do on the job (their job descriptions), but also its rationale. To better appreciate the full scale of this revolution, let us consider in the following pages three sectors of the economy, each one having undergone some degree of upheaval: the air transportation industry, the automotive industry, and hospital health care. A comparison of these case studies should help emphasize the universal scope of the problem.

The airline industry

The case of air transportation is interesting for two reasons. First, from a macro-sociological point of view, it is a sector which has undergone relatively rapid deregulation, which in Europe came to completion in early 1997. Deregulation has brought profound change to the industry, including the elimination of some of the key players (Pan Am for example), economic and social tragedies (Air France lost roughly $1.6 billion in 1993, and Iberian Airlines also faced a tough financial crisis), as well as fierce struggles on the part of airline personnel trying to avoid what they felt was a general decline in the conditions under which they are hired, and under which they work. In early 1997, the President of the United States had to intervene to head off a strike at American Airlines, which everyone thought would be a catastrophic event for the American economy. At the same time, mergers and joint-operating agreements have reconfigured the global air transportation industry: an environment in which each company is in a battle to survive.

From a micro-sociological perspective, we are dealing with a business in which technical constraints have always been the number one concern. This is due to the nature of the business and of course for safety reasons. While the planes are on the ground, there are carefully codified maintenance procedures carried out on a precise schedule by ground crews; in the air, there are very specific security guidelines – nothing is left to chance. A large company would have a hard time surviving a catastrophe for which it is to some degree responsible. As a result, safety is never a part of an air carrier's sales pitch; it is simply taken for granted throughout the industry.

This fact has had far-reaching effects on the organization. If we just consider in-flight attendants, their traditional role was more focused on safety than on customer service – even if these two roles are not contradictory – and this focus has structured their relationship with the customer, just as in the earlier case of the railroad company. It puts the flight attendant in a position of superiority, somewhat like a doctor, whose symbol is the seatbelt: passengers are requested to remain seated with their seatbelts fastened, although they may not really understand the well-foundedness of it all. At the same time, this focus has provided for the attendants a certain number of advantages in terms of rest, rotations, even salary, which is scaled to compensate for the difficulty of their work (jet lag, negative effects of altitude on health), and the pressures of the job (there is no room for careless mistakes). An entire realm of mythical proportions has thus been built up, and airline operations have gone unquestioned for a very long time, operations which force customers to run from this place to that, not unlike what we saw in the case of the university identity card: reservation, check-in, long hours in the terminal, boarding, deplaning, possibly a return to the terminal, the baggage claim. Generally speaking, these tasks are not usually carried out by employees of the same departments within the airline.

Let us now try to disturb this seemingly perfect order by asking a simple question just as we did as we began to explore this branch of the industry: 'How are you organized to manage your passengers (your customers)?' In response, people arrive quickly at the distinction between ground and flight personnel. It is a distinction which surprises no one, probably not even you as you read these lines. And yet, if you ask why there is such a distinction, it will be explained with a smile – at least at first – that since aircraft spend part of their time on the ground and part in the air, it is perfectly normal and hardly questionable that there should be ground personnel and flight personnel. Yet if you push the issue a little further, you will notice that people get a little irritated, a sign that it is truly difficult for bureaucrats to imagine a mode of functioning that is not built around technical constraints. If you really push the matter, people will ask whether you know much about flying, and whether you understand that planes spend part of their time on the ground and part in the air. How will you answer that? That there is no question about that, it is self-evident. Yet you can still dispute the logical jump which was made which seemed perfectly normal and natural to everyone, the jump from the technical constraint that planes are sometimes on the ground and sometimes in the air, to how airlines organize their operations: there are therefore ground and flight personnel. This jump from technical constraints to how things are done lies at the heart of the bureaucracy as we have defined it: and this is what customers are challenging today, not for theoretical or ideological reasons, but simply because, if they can, they will try to get away from any imposed segmentation which costs them in terms of convenience.

Two observations stand out as we consider a real customer rather than just a statistical one. Do customers enter a travel agency asking to buy a little ground, a flight, then a little more ground to retrieve their luggage? Although putting it this way may sound a bit childish, it allows us to emphasize that technical segmentation is not devised by the customers, who from their perspective are buying a trip, a concept which would integrate the different technical aspects. Even better: in air travel, the points at which the customer is particularly nervous or anxious occur precisely at moments of abrupt change between the ground and the flight. Although the segmentation of tasks is the company's solution, it becomes a real problem for customers: the trip to the terminal is slow and unpleasant, there are delays at the baggage claim area and fear that bags might be lost, travellers experience anxiety over missed connections and so on. In a classic airline bureaucracy, when a customer asks a flight attendant 'What do I do next?' the response is at best 'Our ground personnel are there to help you', and at worst 'That's not our job.'

To take this image even further, consider passengers boarding a French domestic airline, an airline which does not book seat reservations. As they wait to board the plane holding passes bearing a letter corresponding to the order in which they board, passengers are so anxious – worried about finding a good seat in an uncomfortable plane – that they lose all notion of civility. They glare at each other, hiding their passes, and jostle the passengers in front of them; in short, they undergo a mini-nightmare which, ultimately, will cost the company a great deal. Since the company did not listen to its customers, many of them will switch over to the competition.

Is it possible to think differently about these issues? As the century draws to a close, one airline, British Airways, stands out for its outstanding financial success. Indeed, the British airline began its revolution well ahead of its European sisters. Interestingly, British Airways' revolution was not just about cutting costs. So that cost reductions would not impact on overall quality, which would in the end have had a negative effect on the company, it redesigned its way of doing business around a concept – specifically, around a careful analysis and understanding of the many contradictory demands of its customers – a concept which is at odds with the bureaucratic segmentation around tasks. So-called 'seamless travelling' is an attempt to erase as much as possible the abrupt changes in air travel discussed above. The company first had to understand what the customer was experiencing, then had to learn to go beyond the contradictions and the fact that the customer always wants more (more comfort, more space, better meals and so on). It could thus get away from its strict form of management control. Next, the concept had to take shape, not in advertising, which is a simple matter, nor even in the behaviour of individual company representatives, which is also not difficult, but in the whole range of ways in which the company operates, its modes of functioning, which is another problem altogether. Let us turn to a few examples which are perhaps not limited to the company in question, but which show the clear link between listening to the customer and a company's mode of functioning.

Until quite recently, what remained of air travel regulation in Europe prohibited an airline from offering service between two third-party nations (which is still the case in the United States). In concrete terms, then, British Airways could not offer potential French customers a direct flight from Paris to Hong Kong. In order to woo these potential customers, the airline would not only have to offer attractive perks (an upgrade in one direction on a round-trip ticket) but also to provide service from Paris to London and back at no additional cost. That would mean accepting a loss in one region (Europe) so as to make an even greater gain in another (Asia). This kind of gamble would be almost unthinkable in the compartmentalized scenario in which individuals focus on their own profits with little concern for the overall organization, and with neither the interest nor the ability to co-operate with each other.

Furthermore, for the French customer to be willing to travel the extra distance, the connections in London must be as quick as possible. To save time during the connection, passengers will have to register their luggage at the initial departure point (Paris), and will consequently worry whether the airline can handle transferring their bags to the second plane in perhaps as little as 30 minutes. They will not be satisfied by some oral confirmation: 'There's no problem, your luggage will make it.' Customers need some kind of follow-up, some proof before boarding the second plane in the connecting airport that their bags have been transferred. This is an extremely delicate matter to handle, for it presupposes that bags will be loaded into the plane's hold in Paris with the knowledge that they will have high priority in London; the ground crews must be able to get the bags quickly from plane to plane; and there must be an efficient computerized system which, as the passengers head towards the gate, will inform them that their suitcases have been safely transferred to the second aircraft. 'Seamless travelling', then, is this kind of operation, relying both on co-operation between people, on methods of working which are based on the customer's way of thinking (the loading of baggage as a function of the connection and not some technical or bureaucratic criteria), and on a uniform, high-performance information system which makes real and tangible for the customer the integration of services and employees, who, by the way, might work apart from one another physically.

Just for comparison, let us briefly consider the very different case of an airline in continental Europe. One employee of this airline suggested that passengers concerned over the whereabouts of their bags should glance out the window and try to spot them as they are being loaded. Focused on helping passengers board the plane, this employee felt unconcerned by an activity that was not within his remit, and with which, in any case, he had no real connection.

One more point: the co-ordination of these operations, which is the 'soft' solution devised by bureaucracies so that each person might be able to remain within his or her own frame of reference, fails to deal with the problem. Liaison employees given the task of co-ordinating the various activities, whether or not they are part of the company's hierarchy, would not have at their disposal the necessary means to integrate and distribute all the information coming from diverse sources. The customer needs co-operation, that is, each employee must be able to enter another's terri-tory, so as to be able to anticipate what is going to happen next, while following up with what has already occurred, and eliminating abrupt breaks in the task at hand. We are beginning to glimpse here how the idea of co-operation, which is the focus of a 'customer-based' orienta-tion, is hardly compatible with our fascination with clear, precise, well-defined structures.

The automobile industry

An analysis of developments in the automobile industry will allow us to proceed even further in two directions: first, how the customer has 'climbed the ladder' to higher levels of bureaucracy, including those which are apparently the most distant; and second, that of the cost of develop-ment or of the production of goods (or services), often seen as a constraint on the ability to satisfy customers, even though lower cost is an integral part of what they want and is a matter of concern to the organizational revolution discussed throughout this book.

Some years ago, the author had several young automobile executives in his seminars, both in Europe and the United States, and he asked them at the start of the session to explain how their business was organized to develop, produce and sell vehicles. The typical response began, 'Oh! It's easy.' This simple utterance is quite significant, in that it came naturally to the lips of these engineers, and tells us that there is only one way of doing things, that the organization is predetermined by, of course, the sequence of tasks to be accomplished. And the description which usually followed fully confirmed this 'ease': the vehicle must first be designed, and so there is the department of research and development. Next, it must be put into production, which gives rise to centralized or decentralized production methods; next follows the vehicle's manufacture, a process which lends its name to the corresponding department, and finally, there is the network in charge of sales and after-market services. This rough sketch does not take into account the other services (the 'product', market studies, human resources), it simply describes the most obvious faces of the organization, which for a long time stood unquestioned, inevitable, logical. The design department is the product; methods, the process. How would it be possible to imagine a process for an as yet unknown product? The product/process distinction is sometimes just as intangible as the ground/flight distinction. One of the large French auto companies provides a good example, where for a long time the product/process distinction has translated into geographical separation (the two entities were located as far apart from each other as possible), and a difference in prestige as well. The distinction has even given rise to vocabulary expressing just how poor the relationships between the two divisions are: those in charge of delivering files [*sic!*] from one to another are called 'mailmen', who are supposed to deliver the mail without being in a position to know or explain the contents.

Of course, the division of departments is reproduced within departments as well. If a vehicle has an engine and a body, reason enough to subdivide the methods accordingly. And to the degree that the body is in sheet metal which has to be stamped out and then assembled, there is necessarily a stamping department and an assembly department. Were we to give each one of these a number, some kind of code which would have meaning only for the system's insiders, we would have an ill-sorted set which we could call 'bureaucratically vague', in which, as we will see, the job of co-ordinating the different units is so difficult that only an external supplier is in a position to do it – at a high cost, of course. In light of this, one begins to see how bureaucracy, apparent clarity, compartmentalization and so on are responsible in a big way for increased, excessive costs which customers refuse to pay whenever they have the chance.

Hell is everybody else!

Taking a few steps back now, let us refocus our analysis of this kind of organization on two points:

1. We are dealing with a classic technical bureaucracy, as defined in the preceding pages. There's no point in hiding the fact that we like bureaucracies, provided that we do not run up against them, but are part of them. There are many reasons for this. First, it is a kind of organization that has a clearly visible structure, and we like clarity and security.[15] Behind the idea of clarity, there is protection: if my territory is clearly defined, no one can encroach upon it, it is mine, I have a monopoly over it. I do what I am supposed to do, and I need not worry about the overall consequences, insofar as the organization's underlying principle is that if each person does his or her job properly, the results can only be positive. But above all, the actor is protected from the very thing which is least natural, most difficult, and most costly in human terms: co-operating with others. Over the years sociologists have come up with various images or expressions for this idea: they speak of 'beehive structures', and of the 'fear of face-to-face interactions'.[16] However it might be described, the observation is still the same. Jean-Paul Sartre put it brilliantly: 'Hell is everybody else!' In the Sartrian sense, co-operation leads people into hell, confronting them forcibly with another way of thinking, leading them into conflict, bringing them to accept conflicting interests and compromise, whereas the rhetoric of daily life (the business place) promotes a 'shared vision', consensus, common goals and common means. This is a harrowing paradox, and is precisely the reason why bureaucracies are, from the point of view of their members, a wonderful solution to the universal question: 'How can we live together without having to co-operate?' And thus instead of troublesome co-operation there is the process, the procedures, the rules, the sequence of tasks, and one time-consuming co-ordinating meeting after another, something in which bureaucrats excel.[17]

   We have already glimpsed that the abundance of means is itself a means of escaping co-operation. If, back at home after a long day's work, a married couple want to watch different television programmes, there are two ways to resolve the problem: either through non-co-operation, in which case they need two television sets and the abundance of means does away with the necessity of negotiation, and thus of conflict; or through co-operation, although of course that will be more 'costly' in human terms. However surprising, it is a perfectly natural result that an organization built around the customer, that is, in which people co-operate (as we saw earlier in the case of the air transportation industry and as we will again see later on in the case of the automobile industry), is more efficient in the use of means than an organization built on the segmentation of technical tasks, which allows its members to avoid co-operation. Not only do customers ask that we operate at lowest cost, but they provide us with the means to do it! It should now be evident why for our third example we will turn to hospitals and the management of the high cost of health care.

2. But that is not all, especially in terms of the problem of cost. If the division of tasks, accompanied by procedures which clearly specify what employees must do, is supposed to provide customers with the goods or services which they have the right to expect,[18] in reality, this is not at all the case. With less co-operation, employees come up with their own rationales, always justifiable given the specialized technical angle from which they view the situation, and the more it will be necessary at some point to make adjustments. This is what in the automobile industry and elsewhere is called 'modifications'. These become more and more frequent as a weakly integrated process goes on, sometimes attaining simply astounding proportions. They run right through the organization, up to the point where they involve the customer either directly, in which case they are called 'weaknesses' in the system, or indirectly and are then translated into a price increase and/or delays in production. Quality, cost, delay (QCD): these form the 'concept' of the automobile industry, just as seamless travelling was that of British Airways. Clearly, so long as customers have no choice, they are given to accept the degradation of this trio (QCD), but as soon as they can, they ask for more, that is, higher quality at lower cost. What does this mean? What is a modification, not in the technical sense, but from a sociological perspective? It is the cost which an organization requires its customers to pay so as to permit its members to avoid co-operation. A modification is a way of regulating this system, that is, the key element around which employees adjust their strategies of autonomy and avoidance, the cost of which they pass along to the customer whenever possible.

It should be clear that we are not speaking here of those who work directly with the final consumer, but of all those who produce value for this consumer, under the terms specified above (QCD), regardless of where they might be located within the organization, even as high up as the research department, for example. In this scenario, listening to the customer means the end of the bureaucracy as a way of doing business characterized by the pre-eminence of a technical rationale over co-operation. Whenever it is said or written that the customer must and will climb high within the organization, it is not just an abstract figure of speech. What good would it do to convince employees that the customer is important, which would amount to little more than a rhetorical exercise with little practical impact? We must identify in concrete terms the consequences for each person involved, that is to say in terms of how people work (modes of work). This was done progressively in the automobile industry, first by setting up transverse operations, called 'projects'.[19] These consist in giving a project leader the job of integrating the work of everyone involved in the concept or production of a vehicle, part of a vehicle, or of a component. Freed from their 'occupations' in the 'projects', engineers, executives and technicians were supposed to work together towards a common goal. This first breakthrough towards complexity over the expensive simplicity of a sequence of technical tasks nevertheless ran up against an obstacle. The initial assumption was that co-operation would result naturally through individual goodwill, through employee interest in working on a project, and/or the project leader's ability to win everyone over by his or her charisma or conviction.

This somewhat naïve vision has not stood up to the facts. Co-operation, like any other human behaviour, cannot be decreed, it must be created. We will try in the second part of this work to offer several possibilities for making co-operation possible. For the time being, let us just say that it was necessary as time went on to bestow on project leaders real means for getting work done, in particular in terms of controlling how budgetary resources are distributed, and how project members are evaluated, so as to get them to work together. At the same time, as we have said before, the organization has today become more complex, more vague according to its members: the vehicle or component projects are intertwined and encroach upon 'occupations', repositories of technical expertise. It has also become more subject to conflict, less comfortable, but at the same time much more lively and 'negotiative'. This conflict was difficult to accept for a long time, especially in France, a country in which open confrontation over differing interests is considered incompatible with the defence of common interests.[20] Elsewhere, on the contrary, this confrontation has been considered not only as one of the conditions of success, but even as one of the keys to its continuance: 'the best businesses have good results because they work hard to build coherence among widely differing and often conflicting interests. It is like a good marriage: a couple enjoy lasting happiness because they have worked to build it: a labor of love, but labor all the same.'[21] Today, accepting this conflict is no longer questioned on principle. It is simply a consequence of customers' presence within bureaucracies which had traditionally kept them on the outside.

Integration and cost cutting

Similarly, new problems have arisen which traditional bureaucratic methods of management have been unable to handle. This is especially the case in people management – human resource management – a mainspring in the transformation of bureaucracies.[22] The distribution of resources between different projects and occupations, the methods of evaluating employees – key factors in co-operation, as we said – and career management, have all had to be reanalysed. Organizations have had to learn to manage their crucial problems more openly, more 'opportunistically', and with less planning. Employees for their part have had to accept greater risk, more unforeseen events, and have had to be more mobile than they would have had they been able to continue along more familiar paths.

Finally, and without suggesting that we are at the end of the journey, we have had to think the unthinkable – again – and bring together what up till that point belonged to separate, compartmentalized worlds. At Renault, for example, on platforms designed for the purpose, design and methods plan the product and the process simultaneously instead of one after the other. This is nothing but the most visible and meaningful face of the very deep revolution which is affecting companies' modes of functioning. Of course, what we really want to know is how this affects the customer. There are two possible answers: first of all, exact figures held by carmakers clearly show that the number of modifications decreases considerably as an organization becomes more transverse. As we said, the 'modifications' – those that correspond to a lack in co-operation – are detrimental to QCD. Moreover, and perhaps more convincingly, the integration that brings together different ways of thinking provides a company with greater control over its suppliers. In the traditional compartmentalized context in which there is no communication, the only ones who in the end have a view of the whole are the suppliers. They are the ones who play the role of 'integrator', taking the place of co-operation. But they play this role only for a price – the price of manipulating information, the modifications game – which allows them, in the end, to send the company an invoice which is well above what was first negotiated in the contract. And of course, there is no way of pinning responsibility on suppliers for these changes. The new modes of work, which bring with them the integration of suppliers at a very high level, today allow them to be more closely controlled, and restores, we might say without fear of exaggeration, freedom within the company.

Once again, one can see in this example the unnecessary cost of 'false clarity'. When we try to foresee everything, plan everything, 'define' everything carefully in advance, we condemn employees to verticality by helping them avoid worrying about others. Others, such as the customers, may worry about this integration, but even this may come at a price.[23] From this standpoint, the way costs are transmitted in organizations is more a problem of functioning than a question of 'economy', in the most basic sense of the term. To say suddenly 'We are cutting 20 per cent off everything' is in a way admitting that we have been unable to implement a real organizational strategy for controlling cost. It is a kind of 'figure it out yourself' mentality, which is only possible when individuals are subjected to pressure which substitutes for a carefully thought out plan of action.

The hospital: less spending, more co-operation

To close a chapter on bureaucracies with a discussion of the health care industry might seem surprising. What can this highly specialized field which is about devotion and real concern for humankind have to do with the pencil-pushing routines of technical organizations forging ahead with their own way of thinking without concern for customers? The link is this: in nearly every nation people are involved in a heated debate over the problem of rising health costs.[24] Yet very few people realize that there is an organizational dimension that must be addressed.[25] Hospitals – which generate the majority of costs in question – can in fact be viewed as the most perfect form of what we have called a technical organization. Because of a need for specialization, which 'customers' are all the more ready to submissively accept since their own health is at stake, a hospital does not really deal in terms of sick people, but in terms of illnesses and body parts, so to speak, and this way of functioning has become quite naturally the hospital's guiding principle. Edgar Morin and Sami Naïr write:

High tech medicine, while producing wonderful results (liver, kidney and heart transplants, the restoration of injuries or war wounds, the reversal of many infectious diseases), suffers from and makes patients suffer from hyperspecialization, according to which the body's organs are viewed as separate from the body, and the body separate from the overall being, be it biological, psychological, or social.[26]

This hyperspecialization does not just pose a human problem, that of 'dissected' patients, as if they were automobiles on the assembly line or in for repair. Hyperspecialization poses the problem of cost for reasons which we have already seen in this chapter. The technical rationale, pushed here to the extreme, allows doctors to avoid co-operating, even getting the patient to help them in avoiding it. The anxiety-provoking nature of the doctor–patient relationship leads the latter to accept and even approve of repetitive exams or treatments. Whenever in public debate people begin to criticize the high cost of these treatments and seek to control them through a purely financial approach – such as forcing doctors to cut down on treatments and prescriptions – practitioners cry wolf and warn of the imminent degradation of public health. Those who are currently sick or potentially sick are quick to join in this outcry. In the end, there is more and more disagreement over solutions, if only because no one has really understood the problem, and there are precious few who actually see the link between the care which they receive and the deficits of a system as abstract as Medicare in the United States or Social Security in Europe.[27]

Thus, health care is really no different from the other organizations which we have already seen. Cost and quality are not really at odds, but so long as they are viewed as such, there will indeed be a decline in benefits in a game in which the stakes are high and everyone loses: as a whole we will only partially be able to control costs, patients will receive care of lower quality, and doctors will experience a drop in their standard of living. The latter, just like everyone else whom we have encountered, are going to have to learn to work differently, in a less segmented fashion, thus less comfortably. They are no doubt going to have to get used to a little less prestige in their particular area of specialization. At the same time, their relationship with patients is going to have to change just as radically as the relationship with the customer in any kind of bureaucracy: this is no doubt where the stakes are highest. This will affect what people actually do at work (their 'occupations') on a daily basis. Readers who find this argument difficult to accept should reflect back to the days, now past, when doctors, by being systematically late, made patients feel all that much more dependent on them. To rebuild the hospital around the patient is not a dream. Not only can it be done, but it should be done, for it would result in improved care at a lower cost. Why would we not treat this particular sector the same as all others, regardless of how difficult it might be for the producers, in this case the doctors?[28] Certain countries have already taken the first steps in this process, either for budgetary reasons as in the United States, or because they are involved in national reconstruction, as in Lebanon, and thus have a chance to rethink the functioning and structure of their health care system.

There is no question that once again we are dealing with a real revolution. For, in countries such as France or Belgium, not only is there the medical bureaucracy, but there is now a bureaucracy that manages health care. In Paris, for instance, women are taken to special hospitals for the birth of extremely premature babies; the premature babies are cared for in entirely separate hospitals. Premature infant delivery and premature infant care are two different 'practices', so to speak, so that in the Institute of Infant Care in Paris,[29] there is not a single maternity bed. The segmentation of health care is thus based on the rationale of the hospital's organizational chart; but as it respects the various specialists, it increases both cost and risk.

More generally, what is being challenged here is the way bureaucrats and politicians go about trying to reduce public expenditures. We had a good example of this way with the case of public transportation. An exclusively financial approach which favours actual 'gross' gains in productivity by simply reducing identifiable costs can only wind up hurting the overall quality of services provided, or might force them to be eliminated altogether. The artificial view that cost and quality are irreconcilable, which stems from a complete misunderstanding of the organizational dimension of the problem, leads many to take a hopeless view of reducing public expenditures, and results in disagreement after disagreement in the debate over how best to go about it. The lack of real debate on these issues, but also the particularly violent reactions which they cause in France, Belgium and Italy, are clear signs that citizens are aware, however vaguely, of the erroneous path on to which they have been lured. In fact, wiser than their own leaders, they cannot understand why the public sector is the only one not to offer improved services at lower cost. From this standpoint, they have entered into the same struggle with government as the customer with the producer. What they want is reform of the state and of the way it operates. Their leaders have yet to make it part of their agenda. Generally speaking, they do not understand what such reform would mean in terms of the organization of public or para-public services. Thus, they make do with traditional approaches to the budget which resolve nothing and displease everyone, and sadly miss a wonderful opportunity to give real meaning to an initiative that would change the way the state and its agencies function. That is unfortunate, since we will all pay for it later on.

Notes

1. Bennis and Nanus (1997), p. 40.
2. Waterman (1995), p. 283.
3. Reich (1992), p. 51.
4. Rifkin (1996), p. 137.
5. Weber (1979).
6. Mintzberg (1982).
7. Burns and Stalker (1961).
8. Fayol (1917).
9. Dupuy and Thoenig (1983).
10. Crozier (1964); see also Crozier *et al.* (1974).
11. Crozier and Friedberg (1994).
12. Taylor (1957). A certain number of Taylor's writings have been assembled and published by L'Institut Renault de la Qualité. On the links between Weber, Taylor and democracy, see Rouze (1993).
13. A simple and accurate presentation of this can be found in Friedberg (1988).
14. Rifkin (1996), p. 81.
15. Cf. Chapter 1.
16. Cf. Crozier (1964).
17. When they speak out against the 'mania for meetings', the members of bureaucracies probably do not realize they are hitting an organization's soft spot. The unending, ever-increasing succession of meetings – today's meetings in preparation for tomorrow's – reveals the contradiction between the increasingly important need to work together (to co-operate) and the impossibility of co-operating in traditional bureaucracies.
18. With some differences however. To paraphrase Henry Ford: Customers can choose any colour car they want, so long as it's black.
19. On this topic, see Midler (1993), p. 244.
20. See Weil (1997).
21. Waterman (1995), p. 16.
22. This is also what Kanter says (1992).
23. A good example of this will be presented in Chapter 4, whereby a company is forced to cover certain costs incurred when it is unable to integrate sales with delivery. The customers are forced to 'integrate' these two divisions, at the cost of considerable inconvenience.
24. See for instance Hassenteufel (1997); also cited in Arnaud (1997).
25. As is the case of Robert H. Waterman; see Waterman (1995), pp. 80–86, the chapter 'And in medicine?'
26. Morin and Naïr (1997), p. 128.
27. On this subject, see Schelling (1974).
28. In a section entitled 'Un new-deal de civilisation', Edgar Morin writes: 'The tremendous advances in health care, especially in the reduction of infant mortality, have nonetheless a dark side. Medical hyperspecialization, the treatment of organs

rather than organisms and organisms rather than persons, the declining role of the generalist, the bureaucratization of hospital services, the increase in iatrogenic illnesses caused by side effects of medicine or by the spread of infections within hospitals, all of this adds a great deal to the cost of health care. Real reform of the medical establishment that entails at the same time reform in the way the biomedical world thinks (avoiding errors and waste) would help to decrease health costs as well' (Morin and Naïr, 1997, p. 15).

29. L'Institut de Puériculture de Paris.

4 A Requiem for Bureaucracy

We enjoy bureaucracies. Those in which we work, that is, not those which we have to confront and which bind us with constraints. We are, in fact, both the bureaucrat and the customer: we apply pressure and we resist it, we demand change and yet we cherish the advantages that are already ours. There is no real contradiction here, as a number of writers have already pointed out.[1] Our ability to play both roles is to a large extent the result of how difficult it is to identify, or 'flesh out' bureaucracy, so to speak, when it is defined in terms of the line of thought governing the implementation of its modes of functioning, and in terms of the employee benefits associated with them. So long as this definition remains relatively abstract and general – the ability to produce general and impersonal rules and to apply them, for example – so long as it underscores the trivial, day-to-day aspects of bureaucracy, just as Balzac described the bureaucrat[2] – paperwork, drawn-out procedures, little contact with others – bureaucracy resembles any large organization, a military model[3] or a form of public administration. And so, bureaucracy is referred to as 'them', even for bureaucrats themselves, who are all the more ready to point out the ungainliness of the world they work in, since doing so allows them to point out their own flexibility.[4]

This is misleading, and it allows businesses in the private sector to preserve a good image by distancing themselves from the public sector. In fact, this distance is not as great as they would like us to think. In order to prove this, we will begin by showing, through several simple examples, that there are as many small bureaucracies as there are large ones, that bureaucracy is not defined by size, that the basic problem is how an organization is conceptualized. From this standpoint, knowing that the elite of the private and public sectors overlap both in the United States and Europe, the modes of thinking are both here and there more or less the same.[5]

Task segmentation

Why not begin with a humorous, albeit striking example of a small bureaucracy as defined here. Step into any ordinary beauty salon – in America or France – and ask for a haircut. Regardless of the kind of salon, the procedure is the same just about everywhere: we are first seated in front of a sink where someone – often a young woman – washes our hair. Then, we are asked to get up and walk over to the stylist's chair. The procedure is so much part and parcel of getting a haircut, that we do not even question it, regardless of how ridiculous we might feel about moving from one place to the next with wet, dishevelled hair, a towel around the shoulders. This very simple organization illustrates one of the most characteristic traits of a Taylorian bureaucracy: movement is applied to the product – in this case, the customer's head – rather than to the workers, who remain at their post.

Let us now attempt to 'interfere with' bureaucracy to see just how firmly anchored it is in the minds of those who never think of questioning it.[6] Instead of acquiescing when asked to get up and leave the sink area, what if we were to refuse, saying that, for goodness' sake, we are quite comfortable right where we are and would rather not have to get out of our chair? The employee will be somewhat bewildered, wondering whether or not we came to the right hairdresser. He or she will explain that in this shop, this is where customers' hair is washed, so that it can then be cut. Well, in that case there's no problem, since that is exactly why we are here. Relieved, our guide will point out that haircuts are given in the chairs, over in the stylists' area. At this point, we explain that we would rather have the stylist join us over here. Increasingly worried, the employee will cite the technical constraints: all the styling tools are kept by the technicians. When we suggest that the technician bring them along, our interlocutor, at wits' end, will hurry over to the reception desk to tell the owner that a 'nutcase' is getting a little out of hand in the shampoo area. What is a 'nutcase'? It is a customer who does not understand the technical constraints, who asserts that they cannot be taken for granted as universal, scientific principles. Here we are again in fully fledged Taylorism, despite the organization's small size, which like all bureaucracies, 'breaks the customer up' as a function of its own tasks and the sequence in which they must be performed. The shampooer's sink and the stylist's chair, two distinct areas of the beauty salon, are the ground and flight operations of the airline, the product and process of the automobile company. And the fact that today many salons are organized differently, either with technicians who handle a whole set of job tasks in one place, or with small teams who work around customers who stay seated in one place, is but one simple confirmation that alongside the segmentation of tasks lies another way of thinking, another possibility, revealed only if we start with the customers themselves. It is worth noting that this alternative results in a change in the duties of a given job (the stylist is now involved in shampooing), or in new modes of co-operation between members of the organization (small teams work within one area of the salon).

The problem of cost is no different in micro-bureaucracies either. Here is another light-hearted example, which occurred in the United States. A European customer leaves for California where he has been sent for six months. Shortly thereafter, he is joined by his wife and children. Just before returning to Europe, his wife decides to purchase a bed quilt, which in her view are of better quality in America than in the Old World. The two head for a small specialty shop advertised in a local newspaper to make a purchase. Upon entering, they are greeted with a smile by a young woman, wearing a name tag. She introduces herself and asks what the couple might be looking for. The prospective buyers explain what they want, and, with the help of the very sincere and considerate employee, decide upon a particular brand and make. Unfortunately, the quilt in question is out of stock, and so the saleswoman explains that they can have it delivered. Learning that the couple plan to leave the country in a short while, which becomes a decisive condition for delivery, she has them fill out three forms – one yellow, one green and one pink – which, according to the employee, will ensure timely delivery of the quilt. The customers and saleswoman say good-bye, everyone in a good mood and quite pleased with the transaction. Yet, the fateful day arrives, and the delivery does not take place. The couple, a little concerned, hurry back to the store where they are received by a different young lady in precisely the same manner as the one before: a sign that the warm, friendly welcome is little more than standardized company protocol. The Europeans interrupt the welcome, stating that they have had a problem with a delivery, the very thought of which, in a country where lawsuits and lawyers reign supreme, could pose a serious threat. After hearing the customers out, the employee regains her smile and almost childishly suggests that they must have made a mistake in filling out the delivery papers. Upon presentation, these papers turn out to be in perfect order, which enables the saleswoman, increasingly relieved, to again declare that there is no problem. The customers, on the other hand, increasingly worried, respond that there is a very serious problem indeed since they have not received the order and are leaving the country the very next day. The saleswoman explains that as far as she is concerned everything is in order, and, of course, the situation is all the less resolved.

What can be gleaned from the preceding sketch? The employee's responsibility clearly ends with the sales order, and, so long as everything has been taken care of in that respect, everything having been done according to the specific procedures governing her functions, there is indeed no problem. Of course in this case the term 'problem' does not apply to the customer, but to the organization; and, insofar as each task is distinct from any other, and since no one co-operates nor has in the short run any common interests with anyone else, it applies to the employee herself, who can relax, since she is free from the worry of being penalized. Even if the rules and procedures which she uses lead to disastrous consequences for customers – and thus to the loss of their business – she is herself covered by this set of procedures, which, as in any bureaucracy, safeguard her more than they secure a positive outcome for the customers. The saleswoman is therefore not responsible for the end result which is a problem only for the customers. Once again, they have been 'divided up' by the mini-bureaucracy between the ordering process and delivery, and it is their job to integrate these two distinct parts of the organization. In the end, they will succeed, of course, but just like the automotive suppliers we saw in an earlier example, they will make the organization pay: afraid of a possible legal battle, the company agrees to ship the item to Europe by express mail, an arrangement which costs the small company almost as much as the original quilt. The shop's loss is twofold: on top of the direct cost which is now almost double and which one way or another winds up increasing the cost of other merchandise, there is the cost of lost business.

Therefore, small bureaucracies operate just like large bureaucracies, be they public, industrial or service producers: they are organized around a succession of tasks (here product orders and delivery) and not around the customer. They seek to govern their relationships with the latter through company regulations and a friendly smile rather than through co-operation. The end result is that costs rise, as shown in the preceding example. What is more, these practices wind up 'protecting' members of the bureaucracy, watering down their responsibilities, and no form of management control can resolve the situation. In the end, they upset their customers, who, if they had a choice, would seek an organization built around them, an organization that would go beyond simple individual service, which is increasingly taken for granted anyway. Once again, even within small organizations, which are often thought to be adaptable and flexible, the determining factor is the mode of functioning: small is not necessarily beautiful in the land of the bureaucrats.[7]

The better a teacher you are, the less you teach!

From the outset, I have tried to draw a distinction between a technical way of thinking and the customer's way of thinking. So be it. But, are they really contradictory, or, at the very least, is there not a way to reconcile them, in a final attempt to ward off the coming revolution? The answer to this question will not only show why we are so attached to bureaucracies, but also why our attachment to them is a lost cause.

Let us begin with the extreme end of the spectrum. Some organizations are built so rigidly around their own way of thinking, around their own technical constraints and/or the advantages provided to their own members, that their functioning, the ways they compensate employees – their modes of management in general – act directly against the needs of the customer. A quintessential, rather light-hearted but useful example of this is the French system of public education.[8] This huge 'company' employs over a million people, which to the author's knowledge makes it, along with its Italian counterpart, one of the largest organizations in the world since the dismantling of the Red Army. The teachers who make a career in this system get there by taking national exams which, in anyone's judgement, are extremely difficult. From this point of view, the French education system is a highly selective bureaucracy. After exams, those who succeed are granted privileges, rewards of all kinds which are greater as a function of the difficulty and thus the level of the hurdles which were overcome. Now, contrary to what one might expect, these rewards are rarely monetary: salary differences within the organization are relatively small. Instead, the most highly prized benefits are to have a reduced teaching load and to be able to choose one's own courses. Although the system has not always functioned in the same way, in general, whereas a young, unqualified teacher yet to take a major exam has to teach 22 hours a week of the most difficult classes (a simple adjunct), a tenured colleague with high-school certification enjoys the lighter load of only 18 or 17 hours. The *agrégé*, who has successfully completed a prestigious national exam (the *agrégation*) faces students only 14 hours per week and may even be allowed to select among courses. Typically, these teachers almost always choose to teach preparatory courses for the French *grandes écoles* – often under the pretext that these are the most interesting classes (for themselves of course), but more realistically because the student–teacher relationships in these courses are tempered by the prospect of very serious exams. At the university level, teaching loads drop to seven or even three hours per week, and at the end of the long journey there is even the possibility of not teaching at all, at which point successful professors can finally enjoy hearing colleagues speak of a 'truly successful teaching career'.

Here then is an organization which offers its members the ultimate reward: never having to face the customers and their needs. In classes where one ought to find the most highly qualified, the most seasoned teachers, they are young and inexperienced. Whereas experience should be the guarantee of quality instruction, it is nothing but a way out of the 'front office', seemingly in accordance with a universal principle of elitist organizations: direct contact with customers is to be avoided. And yet the students have no choice. The teachers they receive are not the ones they need but the only ones the bureaucracy can offer once its own internal procedures for selecting employees and allocating resources have been established. No doubt that the bureaucracy in question has come up with a good deal of unquestionable rhetoric which accounts for its own functioning to those on the outside:[9] the necessity of conducting research, involvement in administrative tasks and so on. But clearly, if one wanted to redesign the organization around its actual mission rather than around the needs of its members, the resulting system would bear little resemblance to what is seen today: the assignment of classes, of teaching hours, of localities would be based on different criteria and would result, like the 'night of August Fourth' during the French Revolution, in the end of privileges. This would be a real revolution, although it would not be all that surprising since it occurred in an organization whose official mission is to teach, rather than to offer its most qualified members the chance to teach less with each successive promotion.

It is also interesting to note that in the world of teaching, whatever or wherever it is, we find the same drive towards specialization and compartmentalization as we did in the health system. The current example of French national education may seem humorous or hopeless – but at the other extreme, can we be sure that an American business school is any different? The top professors – or at least those considered to be the best by their peers – where are they sent? To schools offering MBAs, the 'milch-cows' of universities, but these programmes are difficult to teach because of the expectation of young students who will grade their professors. So they usually turn to the so-called 'tailor-made' programmes which are geared to provide a much more informal relationship with participants, and which allow a better grade. Once again, in these American or European institutions, there is a remarkable balkanization of disciplines which forces students to learn about reality bit by bit, subject by subject, knowing that the only way to achieve global understanding is to give in and follow this piecemeal process. Joint teaching is quite rare, difficult to lead, and most are too afraid to even attempt it. Just like the mythical 'pluri-disciplinary studies' about which much is said, but few have actually taught. In short, in business schools as well, co-operation is nothing but a farce. People speak to one other, but everything takes place in a thick layer of fog. It is up to the student – the customer, in the true sense of the term as far as the business schools are concerned – to integrate it all, to piece the whole picture together as a system.

This explains our fondness for bureaucracies: they offer their members the opportunity to work in predictable environments – by following the rules of the game you will be protected from the outside world. They make it possible, at least in the most sophisticated and high-tech bureaucracies, to barricade oneself behind hyper-specialization, so as not to have to worry about the rest, everyone else, neither one's customers and their needs, nor one's co-workers and what they do. This explains why in these new bureaucracies people are so very fond of technology which provides some substantive grounds for specialization, and which, in a way, legitimizes non-co-operation. Protected by their job status, their entry exam, their hard-earned tenure, glued firmly to their computer screens through which they have access to a world without having to ask anything of anyone, bureaucrats are building a world where there is no more need to sit down face to face with customers to iron out the most obvious problems caused by compartmentalized functioning. Everything – courses, grades, exams – is automated, making it impossible to argue, and even if it were, there would be no point in it. There are those today who see looming on the horizon new bureaucracies based upon advances in technology, and it looks like they are right.[10] Just how customers might be able to resist these is as yet unclear.

The contradiction between these two ways of thinking – the technically driven organizations and the market-orientated ones – is not always as obvious as in the example presented above, which almost everyone takes for granted, whatever the explanation. Often, the contradiction more ordinarily appears as a series of actions which, although they seem perfectly natural and justified, even insignificant, when placed end to end so as to make up the concrete 'organization', wind up producing the opposite of what the customer wants. In such a case, the struggle against bureaucracy usually runs up against two obstacles: first, behind the daily routine there are 'privileges', as defined earlier, that is, in terms of the emphasis placed on an organization's own constraints rather than those of the customer; second, to do things differently means that we will have to change the way we think, accepting that there can be several ways of handling a problem, of accomplishing the same mission, a change which, at least at first, is not natural for people caught up in technical, pseudo-scientific routines, and which they fear might weaken them.

The client held as hostage

Let us take a clear-cut example, once again from the airline industry.[11] Say certain customers wish to travel from one European capital to another on a flight which takes about two and a half hours, departing around 6:00 pm. Say they choose to travel with the national airline of the country of their destination. In making the trip, there is a chance that the plane could be on time, but they themselves could arrive late. Such a statement would seem at first to make no sense whatsoever for the airline's technical staff. If the customers' plane is on time, they are on time; if their plane is late, they are late. It is difficult to grasp the difference because, scientifically, there can only be one working definition of an 'on-time' flight. Consequently, we have hit upon one area, at least, where the customers and the provider could be reconciled.

Let us think about this somewhat differently in order to shed some light on the differences between these two ways of thinking and how they affect the bureaucracy's functioning. How does the airline calculate whether a flight is on time or not? It uses the departure time of the aircraft rather than its arrival time. This is a purely internal technical standard, of little interest to customers. They would gladly take off a few minutes late if, for example, a favourable jet stream enabled the plane to make up the delay in the air. Let us go a little further. As we saw, we are dealing with the national airline of the country of destination. The plane touches down around 8:30 pm at the airline's hub. Now, let us suppose it will not take off again before the next morning, and for technical reasons – above all, safety – it needs to undergo a daily inspection. Servicing is not done in the boarding area, but some distance from the terminal building. Insofar as the entire organization is built around the succession of tasks, it follows that this plane, having departed and arrived on time, instead of heading straight for the terminal, will go to the servicing area, taking its passengers with it. Once there, they will wait for a bus which usually belongs to the airport rather than the airline. Getting these two to work together is probably more difficult than working just within the airline. And so, 'it is not our fault, but theirs', is what the impatient passengers will be told by the flight attendants, who themselves can do nothing about it, but who are the only visible link, responsible *de facto* for the entire trip in the eyes of the passengers. Once the bus or buses are full – at the cost of 'abrupt break' in travel which, as we saw earlier, is a real problem for customers – passengers have another wait as the company verifies that a gate is available and that luggage can be quickly transferred. According to company standards, for the bureaucracy itself, its statistics and self-satisfaction – the plane has arrived on time. Mrs Jane Doe who says to the pilot: 'You landed on time, but I'm late!' is clearly just as much of a nutcase as the customer who questioned the procedures of the beauty salon. She is appealing to a global vision which the segmentation of tasks prevents members of the bureaucracy from having and applying. The passenger is late, in concrete terms, but not statistically, since she will get home perhaps a half hour later than expected. To refund those 30 minutes, that is, to make her somehow more 'on time' than the company, implies an alternative, although not necessarily more complicated, way of thinking. What does it mean to be 'on time' for the customer? Obviously not when the plane takes off, nor even when it arrives. More likely it corresponds to the moment the passenger arrives in the terminal building. Some American companies have understood this, and, when necessary, ask their pilots to announce the time passengers can expect to deplane, rather than the time when they think the plane will touch down on the runway.

In fact, the problem for those who like bureaucracy so much is not only in making the definition of an 'on-time' flight work for those to whom they provide services rather than for themselves; there is the greater problem of putting this new definition into practice. For the airline, how it calculates being 'on time' will determine its mode of functioning. Focusing on the customer rather than on the producer means that the succession of tasks will have to be entirely revised (going to the terminal before the servicing area), along with the description of each task (who does what, who announces what, who is responsible for what), perhaps even in how these tasks overlap. This could mean new work schedules, new definitions of rest periods, as well as new methods of employee assessment and review, different forms of compensation and so on. In other words, just as bureaucracies have been able to take advantage of a system based on their own constraints, customers are going to be able to do the same with a system based on their constraints. Fondness for bureaucracy may soon be little more than a memory.

The end of monopolies

Incidentally, the end of monopolies is really what will seal the fate of this affection. Of all organizations, they are the ones most capable of projecting their own constraints, or the consequences of working arrangements set up among their own members, on to their environment. The simple reason is that in their case customers have no choice, they have nowhere else to go, whatever price they would prefer to pay. They cannot win since there is no contest. The situation is even more acute if the monopoly has a captive clientele: not only has it cornered the market, but in addition its 'services' are essential. Doing without them is not a valid option. In theory, this is what distinguishes government health care benefits (European or Canadian Social Security or American Medicare) from the Internal Revenue Service: a well-off beneficiary of Social Security who is dissatisfied with the programme can choose to drop out and seek different forms of health care. Although the choice may be difficult, the beneficiary can still escape monopolistic bureaucracy. There is no chance of this with the IRS: taxpayers cannot choose not to pay taxes simply because they are dissatisfied with the way the programme is run. I will soon modify this statement somewhat, but even here, we can go beyond the economist's simplistic, somewhat archaic definition of a monopoly: a single vendor and several buyers, and propose a sociological interpretation using the concept of externalization, which was developed in the case study of the French ground transport system. A monopoly is an organization – or a system – with the almost unlimited ability to project on to its environment the burden of its constraints and the cost of arrangements set up among its members. It is a little as if, in going out to eat with a friend, you were to ask someone else to pay, a third party who does not partake in the meal. This would make it much easier for the two diners to agree upon a restaurant, since they do not have to foot the bill. In a way, they do not have to co-operate, that is, to negotiate their different interests. This is exactly what a monopolistic situation makes possible. That is why this kind of organization encapuslates one of the most perfect forms of bureaucracy, and its members never give them up with a smile.

But, at the same time, it would be a mistake to think that a monopoly is nothing more than one company or one administrative body operating in a real or virtual market. There are monopolies within almost every organization. They are created each time individuals or parts of the organization attempt to clearly define their functions, making sure that they are the only ones to carry out a given task, under the pretext, however false, that if this were not the case, costs would skyrocket. Whenever this situation arises, when, under the pretexts of 'clarity' or of avoiding duplicate functions, internal monopolies in fact appear, they behave just like their market brothers or sisters: they externalize on to the rest of the organization the costs of their internal functioning. Clearly, civil servants are not the only ones fond of bureaucracy. All kinds of 'rational' people also like bureaucracy – the defenders of job definitions of all kinds, zealots of the 'perfect' organizational chart who want to put each part of the organization in a separate box so that once and for all it can be manipulated by its members, even if such a perfect arrangement would never work out.

The preceding discussion also says something about why it is so difficult to change bureaucracy – people are reluctant to give up the advantages of making a third party pay – and why for this reason bureaucracies can only be changed by necessity. For bureaucracy, the customer's victory is a victory because it has extinguished the opportunities for externalization and forces members to find other solutions, which are by definition more difficult insofar as they will now have to split the costs among themselves. This is why the last bureaucracies to initiate their revolution will be those in charge of the kingly functions of the state, and are therefore unlikely to be put on the market. This is, in any case, what they think, but it is all very theoretical, for three reasons.

First, because once again, it is important not to confuse market and economic market: the public organizations we are dealing with here are on the political market. Their customer is the politician and they can impose their way of thinking on to their environment provided it has a minimal negative effect on the elected official, who in the end is accountable for public administration in the eye of electors. The political market is clearly capable of exercising control, as demonstrated in a somewhat callous way by President Reagan, and more discreetly, but firmly, by President Clinton.

Next, there are contact, or what one might call capillarity, effects. Customers are increasingly bothered by the fact that they have to pay for the modes of functioning and the lack of co-operation in traditional bureaucracies since many of the organizations they deal with in their daily lives have undergone profound change. What they once thought was acceptable, legitimate, even natural, becomes intolerable. Above all, they have seen that things can be done differently. They have become critical thinkers, they are more educated, in a way, and it is increasingly tough to get them to believe in 'scientific solutions' which are in fact nothing more than partisan deals.

Finally, the very concept of a market is changing, it is broadening, providing new avenues of choice to customers who had seemed captive. Let us take a closer look at what is going on in the Internal Revenue Service, a government bureaucracy which up till recently seemed off-limits. By way of 'loopholes', advantages granted to this or that taxpayer, exemptions applicable in this or that situation, a fully fledged 'tax market' has been created which, needless to say, only benefits taxpayers in the highest tax brackets. These fiscal delocalization phenomena, however limited in respect to the number of taxpayers who actually use them, are nonetheless signs of the effect globalization has had on 'taxpaying' customers. They are clearly not yet signs of a victory. They show that the battle has begun, and that even those bureaucrats who thought themselves among the most secure are going to have to change their modes of functioning, that is, the ways in which their organization treats those who little by little will no longer be 'slaves' but fully fledged customers.

Co-ordination and co-operation

The most significant characteristics of bureaucracies which we have seen up to this point are, first, the lack of co-operation among members (they protect themselves fiercely from co-operation since it comes at a high human cost) and second, the way bureaucracies project the cost of non-co-operation out on to others (externalization). But what is meant by 'co-operation', and in particular how does it differ from simple co-ordination? As we have already seen, co-ordination is often little more than part of bureaucratic rhetoric with few real consequences for the way they function. Let us return for a moment to Rifkin, who explains how the terms differ in meaning, and points out that one (co-ordination) is destined to disappear in favour of the other (co-operation):[12]

> No group is hit more harshly than mid-level executives, those traditionally in charge of the coordination of ascending and descending exchanges... Time-cutting measures force people to react more quickly and to make hasty decisions so as to remain competitive. In the new realm of the nano-second, the traditional functions of management control and coordination seem unbearably slow and completely unable to respond, in real time, to the speed and volume at which the organization absorbs information.

Further on, he adds:

> The arrival of production technologies makes it possible for information to be dealt with horizontally rather than vertically, which in effect brings down the traditional pyramid of the company in favor of networks functioning in one plane.

This goes back to an earlier, more general comment by Robert Reich:[13]

> The core of a company is increasingly little more than a façade behind which one finds an abundance of decentralized groups and sub-groups which are in

contractual relationships with other equally diffuse work units, throughout the whole world.

Even production and operations specialists, who no doubt remain implicitly attached to the product-centred way of thinking, make the jump, even if, as we will see, there is a great deal of hesitation. In regard to the management of a 'lean production' project, Christer Karlsson and Pär Ahlström write:[14]

> Different aspects of the project are integrated rather than co-ordinated. Rather than co-ordinating different activities and diverse groups of personnel from several functional spheres, employees work together. Direct contact and meetings replace the particular functions and resources related to co-ordination...The team is integrated, which is the result of physical proximity, something which takes place whenever individuals work together in developing a new product.

From these excerpts,[15] we can formulate a better definition of co-operation as opposed to co-ordination, and even understand why it is such a threat to bureaucracies. Co-operation and co-ordination have in common that they concern both macro- and micro-organizations. The size of the group in which they are operative is therefore not a distinguishing factor.

Two features of co-operation work together as a cost-reduction mechanism by changing the way in which the organization's members work together.

First, co-operation does not require a specialized governing body to put it into practice, whereas co-ordination does. It implies direct contact between the different parts, the face-to-face negotiation of decisions, of choices, of action to be taken. Here we go back to the controversy over markets and hierarchies, as first mentioned by Oliver Williamson,[16] and, using his distinction, we could say that co-operation depends on the market, whereas co-ordination depends on the hierarchy, that the first is an adjustment among members, whereas the second is the application of bureaucratic procedures behind which members protect themselves and each other, and which in the end enable them to continue on in their own line of thinking: using specialized vocabulary and transforming every meeting into what Sainte-Beuve described as 'a place where one waits for the previous speaker to have finished before taking the floor'.

But the principal difference is this: co-ordination is sequential, whereas co-operation is simultaneous. Co-ordination implies that tasks will be clear (in appearance, at least), they will take place in succession, and they will be subject to modification as time goes by. So, going back to the example of the airline industry, there is an attempt to 'co-ordinate' the activities of ground and flight personnel insofar as they occur in succession, one after the other. But, in the end, this co-ordination actually prevents individuals from co-operating, from confronting one another, enabling them to remain secure in their verticality. We saw earlier, in the case of the automotive industry in particular, that this approach either wears itself out causing the system to fail, or requires an ever-increasing number of resources to maintain quality products or services.

The simultaneity of co-operation could be a solution – even if only partial – to this problem. It gets individuals to sit down one on one, or more specifically, it means that a flight attendant will have to leave the plane when necessary and assist passengers in the waiting room. It means that the pilot will have to get increasingly involved in ground operations, just as the luggage crew in Hong Kong has to take into account how luggage was loaded many hours earlier in London. At the same time, simultaneity compels the different parties to come to an agreement right then and there. It tears down *de facto* all protective barriers, be it those provided by the clarity of tasks, those created by job descriptions, and perhaps in time, those offered by conditions of employment and job benefits. This description is the exact opposite of bureaucracy, which explains why bureaucrats are so opposed to such changes, but more importantly why co-operation is not the usual mode of functioning. As we said, it is not 'natural' for anyone, because it entails confrontation and conflict, and because in general people prefer avoidance and disinterested consensus. We also see why co-operation cannot simply be proclaimed, it cannot be obtained by some simple proof that it is better to co-operate. It has to be understood by each and every individual. It has to be made possible, rational for those involved, as will be argued in the following section. This is more or less what a Japanese manager meant when he said:

> One of the essential tasks is to create an environment in which all of our employees want to cooperate freely and to make them want to constantly improve themselves. With this in mind, it is essential that we provide them with all kinds of information, regardless of their rank or title. Every employee has the right to consult 'all' information available through our computer networks.[17]

This is a very Japanese approach to getting people interested in co-operation, but it serves as a good starting point for creating a favourable environment for the implementation of new ways for employees to work within their organizations.

Since they do not understand this dimension, which will be developed in detail in Part II, some organizations skip the creation of a favourable environment and attempt to use some more or less sophisticated form of pressure: this is to try to change bureaucracy by force, using bureaucracy against bureaucracy, and in the long run, such a practice seems doomed to failure.[18] This is what Edgar Morin and Sami Naïr describe with zeal in their chapter entitled Libéralisme, démocratie et avenir (Liberalism, democracy and the future): Since the start of the 1980s, in both the private and public sectors, the system has tended to impose increasing harsh forms of 'management'… This is why we are experiencing the very real destabilization of methods of leadership and human resource management.[19] The human resource director cited in Chapter 2 wanted to turn his executives into Olympic heroes…

Indeed, these are the issues facing us, and it would be foolish to claim that it is going to be easy. We know that giving up bureaucratic forms of organization comes at a high cost to individuals, or at least that is what they fear whether they are confronted with the idea, or it is forced upon them. In the author's view, this explains to a great extent the severity of change phenomena, as well as the tendency to back away from these challenges, which only increases the ultimate cost of change. Finally, we see that the lack of a methodological approach and the lack of an understanding of human behaviour within organizations, lead us to draw solutions from draconian and stressful forms of management, which in the end only raise the human cost of the process, therefore solidifying resistance a little more, which in turn requires more pressure, and so on.

A vicious circle is created through resistance to change in which everyone is a loser. If this is the case, is there some other way of approaching the problem, some way to lessen the human cost and create conditions in which change is 'workable' for those involved? The author's response is yes. The approach offered here, as we will see, begins with knowledge and the sharing of knowledge, and culminates in the opportunity to 'think the unthinkable'. We will illustrate the process with examples – case studies – which demonstrate as best as possible how it might be applied in the real world. They will help us see that nothing is predetermined, and provided that we are able to think about reality in new ways, that we can show others how to do likewise, and that we can be more confident about everyone's ability to come up with solutions, then, even the most 'case-hardened' bureaucracies should be able to generate and put into practice their own possibilities for change.

Notes

1. Schelling (1974).
2. Bisaoui-Baron (1978).
3. Reich (1992).
4. Dupuy and Thoenig (1985).
5. Birnbaum *et al.* (1978); also Thoenig (1973) and Suleiman (1979).
6. This is taken from an actual experiment conducted as part of consulting work requested by a large cosmetics company. We will return to this example in Part II.
7. Just as many are beginning to realize; see, for example, Izraëlewicz (1997a).
8. Michel Crozier went so far as to claim a few years ago that this organization was so very turned in upon itself and incapable of self-reform that nothing short of a change in the environment was required (the customer's victory suggested by this book I might add) before there could be any hope of change; see Crozier (1979).
9. This is, moreover, what happens when a bureaucracy is attacked. A good example occurred in France when a Prime Minister called state employees 'spoiled brats', referring to their job security. See, for example, *Le Monde* (1984).
10. Edgar Morin writes, 'Our democracies are correlatively confronted with a huge problem, resulting from the growth of the enormous machine in which science, technology, and bureaucracy are intimately connected. This enormous machine does not only produce knowledge and education, it also produces ignorance and blindness. The development of various scientific disciplines has brought with it not only the advantages of the division of work, but also the problems of over-specialization, of compartmentalization, and of the partitioning of knowledge' (Morin and Naïr, 1997, p. 160).
11. *Financial Times* (1995).
12. Rifkin (1996), pp. 146–7.
13. Reich (1992); cited also in Morin and Naïr (1997), p. 56.
14. Karlsson and Ahlström (1996).
15. Nevertheless, as we have argued, there still exists a great deal of confusion between co-ordination and co-operation; see, for example, Song *et al.* (1997).
16. Williamson (1975); see also: Ouchi (1977), Williamson and Ouchi (1981) and Moulet (1982), pp. 484–90.
17. Kagono *et al.* (1985), pp. 112–13 (cited in Rifkin, 1996, p. 142).
18. Cf. Parker and Slaughter (1988), p. 37ff.
19. Morin and Naïr (1997), p. 127.

Part II
THE PROCESS

5 On the Difficulty of Change and its Management

The characteristics which we have found in bureaucracy – in techno-bureaucracy more specifically – are part of a single system. This means that they are in harmony, that they reinforce and strengthen each other, making it extremely difficult and dangerous to define and then initiate a process of managed change. This explains why the body of literature on the subject of change is so abundant and diverse, as we will see later on, as well as why leaders are constantly engaged in a quest for a 'philosopher's stone', for a recipe which would with a minimum of risk spell out what to do, so as to make change acceptable to the workforce and to control its effects as it is being implemented. To better understand the scope of this problem, let us summarize through the five points listed below what is at the core of today's bureaucracies, and which is going to have to change under the pressure from the customer, if they are to avoid disappearing or imploding, taking a needlessly heavy human toll:

- Compartmentalization and verticality, the result of a technical way of thinking concerning specialized divisions and tasks.
- Clarity, considered a virtue in and of itself, but which, as we have seen, results in the creation of internal monopolies, and finally in the members' ability to manipulate the organization.
- Non-co-operation, which resolves the individual problem of confronting others, but at the same time makes the functioning of the collective unit much more expensive.
- Endogenous criteria for personnel management, that is, defined in terms of the constraints on the members of the organization themselves and not in terms of the organization's overall mission.
- Finally, externalization phenomena, which engulf and make possible the first four characteristics which have just been described by forcing the environment, that is, the customer, to pay the associated costs – costs which are not exclusively financial.

One does change a winning team!

The logical question is then as follows: is there any reasonable hope of 'unravelling' a bureaucracy outside of a major crisis serious enough to legitimize change and authorize bold gestures which would be unthinkable in ordinary times? The term 'unravel' is used to emphasize the complexity of the task, for the systemic nature of bureaucracies – the coherence of their structures, the ways they hire, their principles of employee review, remuneration and promotion, their collective ability to resist temptation to change 'smoothly', but also their knack for digesting reforms, thereby cancelling out their effects[1] – gives the appearance of a billiard ball: where does one begin? Which is, paradoxically, a question which bureaucrats themselves ponder quite seriously. It leads them most often to a global vision of change: change can only take place if the entire system is changed, through an overall programme, in which, preferably, everything has been anticipated, anticipated and pinned down. In so doing, in light of what has just been said, we condemn ourselves to immobilism and ultimately cynicism: how could we one day manage to succeed where so many others have failed? We might as well throw in the sponge now, deal with what is most urgent and a turnover of leaders will do the rest. Woe is them who happen to be in office when everything goes to pieces!

Leaders often feel that their own willingness to change runs up against the hopeless conservatism of their troops;[2] these same troops complain that so long as those at the top exhibit such staunch immobilism, it will be very difficult to get the least bit of change underway. It is on the subject of mechanisms like these that Chris Argyris speaks of 'organizational defense routines'.[3] Yet others, whom we might consider rather optimistic, see in the endless debate over change, the need for it, and the efforts to resist it, that the process has actually begun: 'A change in direction often begins when a sufficient number of people talk about it, before really knowing what it is', write Waterman *et al.*[4] Experience makes one a little sceptical about such a statement.

In a larger sense, the breadth of the literature is proof of this controversy and of the uncertainty over how to proceed. There is no need to review this literature here, new or old.[5] Let us limit the analysis to an inventory of some of the terms used in this debate, pointing out a certain number of misconceptions, as well as the issues on which there is some agreement: the importance of knowledge – of listening – when at last one really wants to influence organizations.

First, what legitimizes change, which most authors agree is quite unnatural? In a word, 'crisis': difficulty, dysfunction and, usually, emergency. Erhard Friedberg writes: 'In short, change is always "impossible" in organizations, large or small, and there are always a thousand good reasons not to change, so as not to destabilize the pillars of present functioning.'[6] And a sports coach might add, 'there's no point in changing a winning team'. People only tend to question their own way of doing things if something has gone wrong, and there is no other choice. This underscores the reactive, rather than proactive, nature of change. It is rarely a step taken to anticipate, or even accompany, the transformation of one's environment. It is almost always a reaction to symptoms which must first become quite severe before they trigger a response. To 'not change a winning team' indeed means that even if the team is playing poorly, even if it shows some obvious signs of weakness, victory, however temporary it may be, is reason enough to keep the team just as it is. 'It is still our policy to intervene only in an emergency', affirms a high-level French government employee,[7] a former union member, who was present during the reconversion of regional economies in decline and of industries in transformation.

When this is not the case, and one wants to disrupt a group which seems to be doing well, there is surprise and suspicion. When the manager of the French judo team, an Olympic discipline in which France has performed brilliantly for many years, declared: 'We are changing a winning team', the story was given half a page in the national sports daily.[8] The journalist asked the judo manager something akin to what corporate managers the world over ask themselves every day: 'France has been successful in judo for a long time now. Do you have a recipe for miracles?' His response: 'Never be satisfied. If something works, it must be broken, otherwise you will be stuck in a routine. In contrast to many sports leagues, we are ready to change a winning team. This is judo. This is a world in which one is constantly fighting. If you let yourself settle into a routine, you're dead. At best you're behind everyone else.'[9] Basically, Rozabeth Moss Kanter is saying exactly the same thing when she calls on American leaders to begin to question how they do things before it is too late.[10] On the question of legitimizing change, the author had a personal experience when the head of a large successful international company, number one in its market, asked him to work with the organization to help it adapt to what he saw as its future mission. As powerful as this leader was at the time, he was never able to mobilize the enthusiasm of his executive staff for the process, including those closest to him. Everyone protested, citing the company's excellent performance.[11]

The problem of legitimizing change in anticipation of the future, of initiating and implementing change at a time when the storm clouds looming over the horizon are not concretely visible by any of actors, would seem to explain the current fascination for the 'leaders' and their 'vision'. We will return to this approach later on, which, in the author's opinion, is in part a false hope. But it does underscore the paradox of modern organizations in which no one has enough freedom of movement to be able to affect anything so long as 'indicators' are good, whereas it would be better to prepare, anticipate and take advantage of good weather to begin to work on what will later have to be done amid noise and fury. Since change cannot be justified 'concretely', we call upon this 'world beyond', unseen by common mortals, known as 'vision'. And, we might add, this faith in the leader's 'vision' and leadership stands in the way of confidence which could be placed in members of the organization to help get a process of change rolling, but also – why not? – to help carry it through to a successful conclusion. Unfortunately, confidence is not part of elitist culture, nor, by systemic extension, that of the troops. Everyone is used to turning towards the leaders and their knowledge in normal circumstances, or their vision in times of crisis. Yet, did any one not notice that in the case of Air France, it required a long, hard, painful strike, in which strikers went so far as to blockade runways, that is, attacking the tools of the industry, before the first real process of change undertaken by the company could seem legitimate? And, having been at the heart of this process, the author can attest to how the employees' participation in defining 'doing things differently', in understanding how necessary it was, and in implementing change, were all key factors to success. This only came about when the turn of events made it absolutely necessary!

Once the necessity to change has been understood and accepted, the problem is far from resolved. Is it necessary, as suggested by Michel Crozier in his latest work, to start at the top – although he is dealing specifically with the French case – since the inability of the top to understand what is happening hurts the ability of the whole collective unit to evolve?[12] On the other hand, must change be undertaken 'in factories or departments far from Company Headquarters', as suggested by other authors,[13] which can then be spread through capillary action? The answer depends of course largely on the context. We are led to take one more step and observe, going back to the systemic dimension of bureaucracy discussed earlier, that change is also systemic. We will see later on[14] that this can be thought of not only in terms of what actions should be given priority, but in terms of levers, that is, pressure points within the system which, when acted upon, can be expected to reinforce one another and result in change.

Is change for individuals or for organizations? In other words, should people be changed, their 'psychology', their 'mentality', and then organizations will evolve, or do organizations – here more or less likened to structure – have to be transformed first, and individuals will adapt to them? Beer *et al.* believe that the first strategy is doomed to failure, that it is even one of the principal factors of immobilism. They write:[15]

> Most programs of change don't work because they are built upon a theory which is fundamentally wrong. The theory explains, in fact, that a change in individual attitudes leads to a more general evolution in behaviour. One change in behaviour, repeated over and over hundreds of times by different people, in the end echoes throughout the organization. According to this model, change is like religious conversion. All one has to do is instill the 'right religion' in people and changes in behaviour will follow immediately... This theory is the exact opposite of a process of change. In fact, individual behaviour is strongly shaped by the role which the individual is given to play within the company. The most efficient way of modifying behaviour is therefore to place individuals within a new organizational context.

Experience seems to bear these authors out, and in the following pages, I will try to provide the tools which will help build this 'new organizational context'. Still, other approaches advocate first combining these two levels, one of a personal transformation and the other of an organizational transformation,[16] while stressing that it is individual transformation which brings about organizational transformation. In the author's view, this tends to increase the burden of responsibility for necessary change on individuals, on their psychology or goodwill, as a function of our inability to comprehend the complexity of the situations in which they work, thus, the systems: 'The overlapping of situations and of the positions of individuals must also be understood to account for observed opposition to change. What we might call "obstructions" in the company, are in many cases nothing more than the result of an insufficiently detailed analysis of the contradictory characteristics of individuals', write Fitoussi and Rosanvallon.[17] Clearly, however disturbing or surprising this might be, it is less a question of asking this or that group to change its attitude or disposition, to behave differently, than of finding the organizational levers which would allow them to behave differently. If change – in organizations, of course – were a question of individual psychology or attitude of mind, its implementation would be all the more uncertain and unlikely to succeed. When, in the following chapter, it will be demonstrated that the actors do what they do because they are intelligent – in the sociological sense – that in the end it is not a problem of human stupidity but of intelligence, we will not be embarking on some journey of naïve optimism: it will be to underscore how difficult change is (for, all of a sudden, people can no longer be made to believe just anything), as well as to show that it is indeed possible.

Let us listen to and understand the rationality of the actors, its systemic dimension, which will suggest some possible courses of action. And yet if we wish to find these pressure points outside of the kind of comprehensive, megalomaniacal plans of action mentioned above, from experience it seems that there are two unavoidable conditions. The first is that the diagnosis of the problem must be shared. In other words, there must be a minimum level of agreement among organization members on the real nature of the problem which lies underneath the symptoms. This sharing cannot result from spontaneous dialogue, all the actors seated comfortably around a table. It must be nurtured by what we will call 'listening' to the organization, that is, to its members. This is what allows real dialogue, and prevents arguments and finger-pointing which bring processes of change to a sudden halt. The second condition, as stated above, is to have enough confidence in people to be able to ask them, once the problem has been agreed upon, to participate actively and dynamically in the development of solutions. Can we really think that a meeting between a CEO and a consultant, however intelligent they each may be, can really hold a candle to the creativity of the organization's members, if only they could be provided with some meaningful tools? What is more, such an approach legitimizes the subsequent decisions which management is led to make, and which will consecrate the implementation of change.

Dangerous illusions

Turning now to that very question, it seems useful to point out two misconceptions which the author has encountered time and time again when working with leaders or executives of business and public administration: the first involves rules and procedures, the second, leadership.

The problem of rules and procedures was taken up in Chapter 1. We noted, with others, that the definition of an organization cannot be reduced to these alone, and that they are in fact but one of the elements which actors 'play with'. As a result, changing an organization is not about changing structure, even if sometimes that is required; but above all, changing the behaviour of the actors is not about enacting new behavioural standards (from now on, this or that must be done), nor is it about changing or 'reconfiguring' processes (in the future, tasks will be carried out in the following order); nor moreover, is it about applying simple models to a problem which we think we understand (we are out of touch with customers; therefore, we are going to decentralize).

Changing structures

An example serves to illustrate this idea, showing the limitations of 'structuralism' which is running rampant today in the business world. There is a large company, world leader in a market of products and services which interest a full range of customers from individuals to the largest institutions. The company is present in most of the developed nations where it usually dominates the market. Despite its charisma and excellent results, it is so centralized, out of touch, and insensitive to its customers' daily concerns that it is often likened to a government bureaucracy. Aware of the increasing competition, the company president decides to tackle the problem, believed to be the company's estrangement from the customer, and embarks on a programme of decentralization, which is indeed the first thought which comes to mind with respect to drawing nearer to one's customer base. The first steps are quickly taken, systematically, resulting in the creation of structures that are identical in every country where the company is present. Below a national level of management which is to be trimmed of any excess fat, regional levels are planned and set up in which technical business specialists are placed at the customers' service, ready to analyse and respond to their needs. It is thus hoped that both reactivity and the creativeness of the organization will be increased.

However, one or two years later, an element of doubt begins to set in. Not that the reform failed – when the author's firm is asked to evaluate the results, comments emphasize the positive aspects – but the results were largely unexpected. More specifically, everyone complained of increased amounts of work, of an inability to handle requests appropriately, and customers themselves seemed just as ready to switch over to the competition as before reform, if not even more for some of them.

What went wrong? Is the 'listening to the customer = decentralization' equation not as simple as it seems? To put the whole matter in a nutshell, the system, or, in this case, the new structure, did not function as planned. Not that any one seemed unwilling to go along, no more than they seemed to 'resist change'; not that employee 'attitudes of mind' did not change: the resulting problems are more or less the same in each country. More simply, the actors took hold of the new rules, used them, and created a new system whose functioning had not been anticipated. Let us try to outline its main characteristics. The company works with customers both large and small. Through a very efficient publicity campaign, customers are made aware that from now on the company wants to enter into partnership with them, and that from now on the technical consultants are entirely at their service. As a result, customers hurry in with their special requests, problems and detailed questions. The regional level of management is quickly over-whelmed by this influx of business. Very naturally, bureaucratic reflexes kick in: to be overwhelmed means in fact to be free, that is, to be able to choose which questions will be answered and which problems will be dealt with. In an emergency situation, people choose to deal with what is famil-iar, which requires less investment, and which can be resolved as a matter of routine. The remainder, more complex, requiring abilities or solutions which are not immediately available, is at the worst put at the bottom of the pile or at best sent on to regional managers, 'for your review', who are themselves swimming in problems which they are really unable to resolve since they lack the necessary information. This is the classic description of a bureaucratic vicious circle. Customers are capable learners, and very quickly turn this new system to their advantage. They learn that they can take business that is not too complex, that can be handled routinely, to the company. There's a good chance that it will be handled in a timely fashion, and it will be a good deal for them, insofar as the company is 'purchasing' the right which it has granted itself of selecting only the business matters which it wants to deal with. On the other hand, complex business, requir-ing ultimately some innovation – not in the sense of a fundamental tech-nological breakthrough, but in the sense of the ability to find a solution to a problem which cannot be solved as a matter of routine, or through day-to-day procedures – should be taken to the competition. Competitors are better able to deal with this business. Since they are more interested in attracting new customers, they work hard to fill in the gaps which the new organization prevents the company from filling. This is what we can call a 'new system' which goes far beyond some new structure. Three important points stand out in this example.

1. As we said earlier, listening to the customer is not a function or a struc-ture, but a mode of functioning. A mode of functioning is neither decreed nor inscribed in rules and procedures. The latter can help get this new mode up and running if they are used and manipulated by the actors. In the case of the company, this is precisely how the negative effects which we saw were rectified, at least in part: not by relying exclu-sively on decentralization to get back in touch with customers – which

can be thought of as a necessary but not sufficient condition – but by setting up a system for employee review at the levels of the technical specialists and regional managers, which rewarded those who responded to customers' complex business requests. It was necessary to counter-balance the bureaucratic temptation, and human resource management tools proved to be effective levers.

2. We have come full circle to the idea of a system which will be very useful later on. In the process of change initiated by the company, the fact that it was focused on its own organization, its own structure, obscured the cards held by the customers themselves. They are considered passive, or at least predictable, behaving exactly as the organization expects. This is what we might call here the theory of the 'tin soldier'. The customer is carefully aligned, and can be moved about as a function of the outcome we want to give to the battle. But, in reality, things happen quite differently: the idea of structure leads us astray, because it sets up a division between the organization and its environment that seems concrete, but which is in reality artificial and abstract. The two are part of one system, and the customer, once again, is capable of playing within, and with, the new organization. Customers are intelligent, they take it over, select what is in their best interest, what provides the greatest number of opportunities, and so on. From this standpoint, it would be worth pointing out to marketing specialists that the idea of 'use' used to understand how customers appropriate products for themselves, can be applied to the organizations which they make use of in the same way. When it was said in Chapter 2 that what distinguishes competitors is more the kind of organization than the kind of product, this was precisely the kind of phenomenon being referred to.

3. Finally, we have learned something important about innovation. In the modest but realistic sense which we have given it here, it does not usually originate with some genius working away in the laboratory. This should be obvious here. Nor is it the creation of a structure – the board of directors of innovation – nor even of an organization, which, since it is part of the 'real world', might be thought 'better able' to understand the needs of customers, and 'therefore' to respond to them. The 'better able' and the 'therefore' are problematic. What pushes a company to innovate is not just getting in touch with customers, deciding to listen to them and preparing to answer them. It is that the system which is created – following the example given above – will be set up in such a way that customers will see that the best strategy for them is to bring complex requests to the company, and that its customer representatives will want to handle this business first, or send them along to the rest of

their organization where they will be handled with real interest. This is the opposite of the lone scientist, for innovation is no longer a solitary activity, nor is it even the rather idyllic image of 'a team of researchers working away in their laboratory'; it is produced in a system, in the context of a set of relationships which cannot be decreed, which heightens the difficulty of setting them in place. Yet suitable conditions for these relationships can be created, provided that the necessary tools for logical reasoning are available.

Thus, when we speak of the difficulty of change, we are not just talking about what managerial rhetoric calls 'opposition to change', and which would be an individual characteristic, almost always more concerned with others than with oneself. It may be difficult – but it is possible – to construct, one step at a time, human systems which produce the desired effects or at least some of them. Indeed, faced with this difficulty, we could run and hide, burying ourselves in the luxury of careful explanations and precautionary measures which surround the processes set into place. And, when all is said and done, the good decisions having been made, the 'logical' ones, if it does not work out as it should, it is because people are unwilling and are not playing the game. But in fact, the opposite is true. They are playing the game; not in a linear, causal and predictable way, but in way that is intelligent, complex and systemic. This is the dimension in which we must place all of our resources, for therein lies the key to managing change.

Vision and leadership

The question of leadership can be found at the other end of the spectrum of misconceptions, so to speak. Here we leave the realm of rules and procedures for the world of those often quite remarkable individuals, the leaders, with all their skills and practices. Executives the world over are fascinated by these individuals, which is not surprising, and it has been this way since time immemorial. Our difficulty to control what goes on in a company, the uncertainty of our predictions, our imaginary control of realities which are both so complex and changeable that they wind up seeming totally unpredictable, all of this seems to incite us to seek something different, something more powerful, something far beyond ordinary forms of management. It is not for nothing, as we will soon see, that most well-known authors make a clear distinction between the leader and the manager.

This introduction is perhaps a bit exaggerated. Yet it sums up rather well some of the imposing body of literature which has appeared on the subject.[18] Apart from the serious and well-documented works, there is in this trend something reminiscent of gold miners in search of El Dorado. In fact, there is really no point disputing the existence of leaders, who no doubt possess the characteristics which specialists attribute to them[19] and are just as important in the life of an organization as they are purported to be. And yet, one must wonder whether there is anything really useful in this approach for the implementation and management of change, or, in other words, whether what we think we know about leadership is transferable and useful to those who, day in and day out, are in charge of organizations. From this angle, the controversy is extremely confusing, which explains in part the rhetoric and the abstract ideas which are quite influential in companies today.

Let us try to summarize the debate around four points.

1. In common-sense terms, we have all encountered leaders whose success amazed us, whose ability to decide something at just the right moment was crucial, and who were able to lead others along the path of success with them at a time when virtually everyone thought the situation was hopeless. Lee Iacocca of Chrysler Corporation and Christian Blanc of Air France are two good examples of this vision; no one could really unravel the mysterious alchemy of the exact circumstances, the context and their personal qualities. They represent 'history' in the sense of a story, a 'success story' which we all admire, but, even if people talk openly about their 'method', it is quite unlikely that they could be imitated.

2. In a larger sense, it should come as no surprise that leadership is sometimes necessary to bring about change in organizations. Erhard Friedberg calls the leader 'the entrepreneur of change', the key figure who has both the interest in and the power to implement the transformations, as well as the personal qualities to do it no doubt, but which in truth depend much more on the context than on any particular intrinsic qualities. Friedberg emphasizes rightly that the job of the leader is more to create a dynamic, thus to make the initial decisions, than to have in mind clear final objectives. In a way, leaders are people who can mobilize the means to uncertain ends. It is then their responsibility to get the organization back on the right track.[20] This approach seems much more concrete and pragmatic insofar as it makes knowledge (the initial diagnosis) one of the conditions which enable executives to take the risk of change, and then become leaders. Here we get away from the hype and

get back to what is really possible. We will take one more look at this in the chapter to follow.

3. But the rhetoric of leadership takes a risky step forward whenever it moves insidiously from the observation of the existence or necessity of leadership, to the possibility or even the obligation that everyone must put it into practice. Admittedly, this jump has had some usefulness in business, since this is what created the leadership market in which so many have become ensnared.[21] But it opens out on to descriptions of leaders and of what to do to become one which look like little more than sophisticated horoscopes: they are sufficiently broad and general so as to cover the whole range of possibilities, and are thus of no real use.

4. Finally the dream of transferability runs into a contradiction which could destroy the leader concept altogether. The practices of leaders are marketed and taught so that everyone can attain that status, but at the same time, if that were possible, then we would no longer be dealing with leadership but with management! It would become simply one more specialized division, just like finance, marketing or management control. And yet, it has been practically the obsession of some of the most popular authors to try to clearly distinguish between the leader and the manager. In their latest work, Bennis and Nanus write: 'The distinctive role of leadership (especially in a volatile environment) is the search for "knowing why" before "knowing how". And this distinction illustrates, once again, one of the key differences between leaders and managers.'[22]

What stands out from this quotation is not the rhetorical debate over leader and manager, but the importance placed on knowing why, that is, on knowledge. This is actually one key point on which authors of different viewpoints agree. Only, unlike the sometimes overly zealous theoreticians of leadership, it seems more likely that the 'knowing why' – once again the understanding of the problem or problems – is something which can be acquired given an appropriate logical framework:

- Beer *et al.* note that to bring about a satisfactory mobilization and to involve teams more fully in the process of change, the diagnosis of the organization's problems must be voiced jointly by all those involved.[23]
- Chris Argyris speaks of 'knowledge for action' and distinguishes between usable knowledge and useful knowledge.[24]
- Michel Crozier places in the forefront of the debate, over the difficulty of change, the inability of the elite to understand reality.[25]

■ Fitoussi and Rosanvallon observe that what is lacking is not willpower, but analysis.[26]

All of them are right: we do not need behavioural or organizational models to change our bureaucrats and our bureaucracies; nor do we need to have a precise or particularly comprehensive idea of where we should be headed. The top-down vision, which constructs a comprehensive plan in which everything is preconceived, is at once over-confident, inapplicable and in the end without effect. What we do need is to improve our knowledge of problems and thus of the reality of the actors and of the organizations in which they work. Access to this knowledge presupposes, as we saw, a frame of reference, its use and a methodology. This, then, will be the focus of the following chapters, which will be illustrated with solid examples, drawn from personal experience.

Notes

1. On this subject, see the excellent special report in *Le Monde,* (1997a), on the ability of French public administration to re-create for itself a little freedom despite the constraints which authorities are trying to impose on them. On the ability of organizations to resist change, see Rifkin (1996), p. 264.
2. This is, for example, the stance taken by the President of France in early 1997. For a reaction – in anticipation of what is to come – to this vision, see Fitoussi and Rosanvallon (1996) – see in particular the section titled 'repenser le réformisme', pp. 185–95.
3. Argyris (1995), pp. 30-65.
4. Waterman *et al.* (1980).
5. The body of literature on this is especially impressive in the United States. Some important works are: Tannenbaum *et al.* (1985), Kanter *et al.* (1992), Nadler *et al.* (1995), Hammer and Champy (1993), Tichy (1983) and Argyris (1995).
6. Friedberg (1993), p. 337.
7. *Le Monde* (1997).
8. *L'Equipe* (1996).
9. *Ibid.*
10. Kanter (1989).
11. Deschamps (1995).
12. Crozier (1995). Note this passage early in the book on p. 8: 'Our elite is on the edge. The less efficient they are, the less they can stand up to criticism. It is literally inconceivable that the government in charge, that leaders of institutions should declare shamelessly that they are unable to bring about the least bit of change because of rigidity, compartmentalization, and conservativism within the company or the organizations they lead...For it is surely high up within the State, in public administration, in the system of the *grandes écoles* and in the senior branches of civil service that the reason for this rigidity and compartmentalization can be found.'
13. Beer *et al.* (1992), pp. 93–103.
14. See the example of the European Bank for Development.

15. Beer *et al.* (1992), p. 95.
16. See, for example, Quinn (1996).
17. Fitoussi and Rosanvallon (1996), p. 187.
18. A complete and sophisticated presentation of much of the debate over the problem of leadership can be found in the collection of 31 papers in Hesselbeim *et al.* (1996).
19. See, for example, Bennis and Nanus (1997).
20. Friedberg (1993), p. 235ff.
21. This is the case of Bennis and Nanus (1997).
22. *Ibid.*, p. 38.
23. Beer *et al.* (1992), p. 97.
24. Argyris (1995).
25. Crozier (1995), and also Crozier (1979).
26. Fitoussi and Rosanvallon (1996), p. 187.

6 The Frame of Reference

Let us begin with the following proposition formulated in the preceding chapter: it is all the more difficult to change an organization when the actors in the organization – leaders as well as employees – have a poor understanding of how it functions. For the leaders, as is often observed, this puts a damper on their ability to make decisions over which they feel, however confusedly, that they have no control. This is what managerial rhetoric calls prudence. Similarly, this leads them to various protection strategies (bluntly called the 'cover your ass syndrome' in America) which determined sociologists have been studying for some time now.[1]

For the members of the organization, this lack of knowledge leads them to behave with mistrust and resistance, heightened by the fact that they do not understand what the problem is that is being dealt with, and that what they are told does not seem to them to correspond to reality – their reality – so that this being the case, for them, change is accompanied by guilt: their former practices are seen to be under fire for no good reason. Consequently, access to knowledge of what we called in Part I 'concreteness', the real organization, is neither the result of scientific aestheticism, nor of some humanistic or philosophical bias. It is a key factor in getting people to both accept and implement change. Moreover, in the preceding chapter, it was pointed out that this is in fact a fundamental point on which authors agree – authors of different cultural backgrounds and of sometimes contradictory points of view.

The problem facing us then is that of carefully working out this knowledge – making a diagnosis – inasmuch as the actors perceive it, even if their perception is of course fragmentary, compartmentalized, disconnected and partisan. What matters is the systemic dimension,[2] that is to say the link between the different parts and between these parts and the whole. It is this added value which is lacking in spontaneous knowledge, in the 'quick glance', however well founded it might be on actual experience. The following examples demonstrate this clearly and explain why the actors in an organization, faced with the results of a sociological diagnosis, can be surprised by the facts presented to them, and yet can accept them provided that a

coherent – systemic – presentation of the facts gives them the real feeling of having been listened to. It comes both as a revelation, and as a release mechanism with respect to the usual practice of dividing reality, cutting it up, classifying it, a practice which for its part, produces problematic side-effects which wind up, with use, locking the system up: the behaviour of each individual, taken alone, is *de facto* linked only to the actor who exhibits it. Behaviour appears as the problem when most often it is only a symptom, and attempts to modify it usually focus on the actor alone. An appeal is made to his or her goodwill, convictions or at best personal interests, meant here in the most basic, mechanistic sense of 'motivation'.

We encountered this kind of organization earlier on, which, overcome by an urgent need to be 'customer-orientated', tries to do so by blaming the attitude of employees who work directly with customers. In so doing, they point a bold finger at the guilty ones – those who must change – and obscure the systemic dimension of their behaviour. No doubt this is the more comfortable, simple solution, but as indicated earlier, in the end, changing employee attitudes only becomes all the more difficult, since they now feel with good reason that no one has even listened to them, that is, that no one has understood the real world in which they work, and within which their actions have meaning. We will see later on, in a particularly striking case study, that some actors support a bureaucratic way of thinking 'by default', since they have no other models, since they believe that tried and true bureaucracy alone can protect them; when they are presented with something else in the name of 'good management', or out of sheer theoretical or ideological criticism of bureaucracy, they rebel, fearing the effects that change might have on themselves and upon the reality which they have worked out for themselves, but which no one has taken the time to understand.[3]

The systemic knowledge proposed here requires a frame of reference, which might also be called a mode of reasoning. Developed on the basis of Herbert Simon's early work on bounded rationality,[4] it has since given rise to heated debate and to an impressive body of literature, which, is not the matter of this book.[5] It will be presented quite simply, beginning with the author's own work in seminars, developed slowly but surely in the hope of making this mode of reasoning available to the actors themselves. Beginning with a seemingly ordinary example, which is in fact extremely rich, we will attempt to answer the burning question at the very heart of the work of both social scientists and managers wishing to undertake change: why, within organizations, do people do what they do and consequently, why do they not do what they are asked to do?

The dilemma of the shampoo girl

The author had the good fortune of working on the following case study. It is hoped that the professionals involved will excuse the way I have presented the facts here, intentionally simplified and adapted for pedagogical reasons.[6] A particular company, world leader in the cosmetics industry, was faced a few years ago with the following question: just like its competitors, the company sold its retail hair products through various distribution networks: supermarkets, specialized shops, drugstores and so on. Traditionally, the beauty salon was not used for direct customer sales. In the salon, the company had only offered so-called 'technical' products, available exclusively to beauticians who could use the products on customers in the shop. Quite naturally, there arose the question of developing specific product lines for beauty salon customers. The company took a major step forward and decided to invest in this new sales initiative.

This was, first of all, a sizeable strategic gamble, insofar as the company had to first create new brand names which would then be offered in competition with existing brands, some of which already bore the company name. But it was a major business opportunity, given the number of potential sales outlets: in France alone there are more than 30 000 active beauty salons, that is to say, individual shops. There was also financial risk, requiring new personnel, display shelves, publicity campaigns and so on.

Once the decision had been made, the company began implementing the plan with its usual efficiency and know-how. Marketing studies were carried out, the products developed and tested, a sales strategy carefully thought out, sales staff recruited and trained, and even though salon owners seemed a little reluctant, in some countries at least, the company's influence and its relationship with the profession, allowed it to attract those whom it considered to be at the heart of the business.

Then, a long way into this great business venture, a particular question arose which on the surface seemed rather unimportant: in the beauty salons, who was going to offer the products to customers? The old theory of how individuals are motivated financially whispered the answer, and, in fact, freed the company from having to take a closer look at the real situation: someone who is paid relatively little wishes to make more (a mechanistic vision of human behaviour within organizations).[7] Certain salon employees fit this description: if, as 'motivation', they are given material, financial or other stimuli, they will begin selling the products, no doubt taking full advantage of the enticements offered them. These actors – the 'shampoo girls' – are generally young, low-paid apprentices who, as such, should see in the new project a good opportunity to increase their monthly earnings.

Let us take a moment to understand in simple terms what mechanistic reasoning is, as opposed to systemic reasoning. The first takes into consideration only two actors, in appearance the only ones directly involved in the problem: the shampooer and the customer, independent of the context in which their relationship takes place. Direct action on one of these actors (the stimulus offered to the shampooer) should thus affect his or her behaviour *vis-à-vis* the other (they will offer products to customers). This approach assumes that the behaviour of these actors is predictable – especially that of the employee, based on a universal model (motivation) – which does away with the need for more careful 'listening' to the salon as an organization. By extension, it can moreover be observed that the use of models – behavioural, organizational and so on – supplants more difficult awareness of reality. Their use is reassuring since it promises solutions, although they are never based on real knowledge of the problem, but on *a priori* hypotheses, on simplistic postulates, or on statements which, after several repetitions, begin to be misconstrued as universal law. This simplistic approach, so typical of the 'substantial' theories of management as they are currently taught in many business schools, is a return to Taylorian unique rationality – if indeed we ever really got away from it. Once the main characteristic of an actor has been identified, how he or she will react in the future is 'known', regardless of the setting – the organization – in which this actor is employed. In so doing, human intelligence, the actor's adaptive ability, and the strategic dimension of his or her behaviour have all been reduced to nothing, but which, as we are about to see through the example of the shampooer, are absolutely essential.

Let us return to the example. A few years after the new sales plan had been implemented, the company conducted its first in-depth analysis which turned out to be rather disappointing: the results were not there, especially in France, and a quick look at the situation reveals why: despite the benefits granted them, the shampooers were very reluctant to offer products to customers. The company redoubled its efforts, offering new forms of enticement as well as increased pressure on sales representatives, and through them on to the shampooers, but these were just as unsuccessful. The reluctance to sell products was just as great, which led the company to conclude, although with a little overstatement here, that the intellectual limitations of the shampoo staff combined with their lack of enthusiasm, prevented them from taking advantage of this opportunity.

And yet, why should the 'intelligence' of an actor be questioned? In fact, to do so reveals that the solution is inadequate, that company decision-makers have not succeeded in understanding the problem, the real

problem, since understanding presupposes a different mode of reasoning, not the application of an abstract, theoretical model.

What mode of reasoning? Let us begin with a simple postulate which we will develop later on: in organizations, as in collective life in general, actors do what they do not because they are dumb, stupid or ill-intentioned, but because they are intelligent. In other words, the problems which we find in organizations are not the result of human stupidity, but human intelligence. Intelligence is not to be understood here as the ability of an elite group forced to understand everything, to control everything, to master and eventually reformulate everything in some kind of perfect formal logic.[8] Rather, it should be understood as the modest ability of the actors, within the specific context in which they work, in the here and now, to find a solution which is, at least as far as they are concerned, the least bad or first acceptable of all possible solutions, however one prefers to say it. This is indeed what Simon called 'bounded rationality', which he contrasts with sole rationality, which applies to the models mentioned above, financial motivation in the case of the shampooers. 'An example is the difference between searching a haystack to find the sharpest needle in it, and searching the haystack to find a needle sharp enough to sew with',[9] write James March and Herbert Simon, decisively establishing with this simple metaphor the difference between sole rationality and bounded rationality.

Let us take a more careful look at March and Simon's proposition: say, one morning, as you are putting on your last clean shirt you notice that a button is missing. In order to sew it back on, you need a needle; and yet you have very little time if you want to make an important meeting. You have at least two possible solutions.

The first, the result of a careful and scientifically flawless analysis, leads you to look for the sharpest possible needle, the one best suited to repairing the button without damaging the shirt. You will then go about looking for the sharpest needle in the haystack – the sewing kit – since this is the scientific solution... and as a result, you will miss your meeting.

The second solution leads you to consider the different constraints: I cannot leave home with a button missing, I have to be on time for my meeting, finding an appropriate needle in a disorderly sewing kit is not easy and so on. At this point, you will not select the best solution (sole rationality), that is, the best in technical terms; rather, you will select the one which will help you solve then and there the contradictory problems of the moment. Perhaps the needle is not the most acceptable, but you did not spend 15 minutes digging for it either, and the button can be reattached in time for you to make your meeting: this is bounded rationality. This is not the abstract 'best technical solution', but the least bad, the first acceptable one. In sociological language, you have unconsciously adopted a rational strategy, which does not mean that you made a correct choice, nor that we must approve of your solution, but which demonstrates the real meaning of 'intelligence' mentioned above.

And so, to help the company make some progress in its hair product sales initiative in salons the world over, the line of reasoning must be turned around, and we must try to understand how the shampoo staff are acting 'intelligently' – as everyone does. There is likely to be a systemic reason why the shampooers choose not to offer these products to customers (strategic dimension) in a world that is much more complicated than the simple one-on-one scenario of the vendor/consumer (systemic dimension). To do this, we have to take the time to piece together the world of the beauty salon in all its complexity, beyond its apparent simplicity, and modestly observe what is happening, letting ourselves be surprised.

Early on in Chapter 4, we observed the Taylorization of this small world, in the fact that as part of the classic production process of the salon, what is moved about is not the worker but the product to be transformed, in this instance the customer's head (movement from the sink to the seat). Let us add that in this compartmentalized world, there are 'rules of the game', as in any organization, that is to say a set of codes of proper behaviour, unwritten of course, which each person must respect in order to survive, or more concretely, to avoid being rejected by the other actors. In a more sophisticated form, this is what we would call 'culture': the set of formal and informal rules which evolve over time, encoding the rights and duties of each person *vis-à-vis* all others. The understanding and acceptance of this 'culture' are both a condition for the sustainability of the organization and a mark of integration.

In the beauty salon, the rule which provides the most structure is the one by which someone belonging to an 'inferior' category in terms of qualifications has no right to discuss with the customer what someone belonging to a 'superior' category does or will do. Put more directly, this means that the shampooers must not discuss with customers the technical aspects of the stylists' or technicians' jobs. If they do, they will face a situation of conflict, which, if it is prolonged, will cause those employees to be fired by the owner who knows it is easier to hire a shampooer than a good technician. Now we have begun to use systemic reasoning. To understand the relationship between the two actors (the shampooer and the customer), and the strategy of one of them (the shampooer's refusal to offer products to the customer), we have had to bring in other members of the organization, who at first glance do not seem directly involved (the technicians and the owner of the salon). Here 'systemic' means that each of these actors develops a strategy – a strategy to preserve autonomy in the case of the technicians – and that these strategies are interconnected, and can only be understood as a whole, not in isolation.

Let us go a little further into the beauty salon, and observe that there are no old shampooers. The reason is obvious: as young apprentices, they have the simple goal of becoming technicians themselves. Either they attain that goal, and continue along the path, or they fail and go on to something else so as not to have to continue shampooing and sweeping the floor the rest of their lives. As we continue developing our frame of reference we will say that they have a 'problem to solve' which is to become a technician. Here 'problem to solve' does not mean to confront a momentary difficulty, but to try to obtain something, and in this pursuit – we have come full circle – the actor develops some rational strategy. This concept is very different from that of 'motivation', the one first used by the company to get its new plan underway. The idea – 'from outside' we might say – that low-paid actors want to make more money is neither true nor false. It is simply useless insofar as these actors have not been heard out in an attempt to understand, beyond general abstract models, what they themselves want concretely when they do what they do in the context in which they find themselves.

Note that, for shampooers – to become technicians, that is – the solution to their problem, is to be promoted. But this profession is just like every other. Promotion requires a minimum level of stability, a certain time in one place, so that employees can demonstrate their professional competency and ability to be integrated into this human world, which is an equally important factor of success. As we said earlier, each conflict between technicians and shampooers will turn against the latter, possibly ending in their departure in search of a new salon, where they will have to start again as apprentices.

Let us now bring in, say, customer Jane Doe, and suppose that, as she makes her way over to the 'sink' area, the shampoo girl offers the line of hair care products. Through careful observation of this interaction we learn that the customer responds to this offer by two highly risky questions insofar as the young shampoo girl is concerned. The first is whether the technician – supposedly the knowledgeable one in the matter – uses these products herself, which of course would make the offer all that more credible. But what can the shampoo girl say if the technician uses a different product, one which she developed herself, for example, in the course of her profession, but which has nothing to do with the one being offered? In fact, to sell a product to the customer, forces the technician into a corner, face to face with the *fait accompli*, making it almost obligatory that she too use the product line. And yet as we saw, the technician tries to preserve her own autonomy, for her own differentiation. Whatever 'backs her into a corner' is going to annoy her, resulting in conflict, and we already saw what the result of that would be.

The second question which the customer might ask after being presented with the line of products concerns the possible effects of the product on her permanent or hair-colour...on whatever work the technician may do. In selling the product, this implies that the shampoo girl will have to field questions with respect to what is going to happen, with respect to what other actors are going to do legitimately, as part of their job, the very ones who deny her that right. Again there is conflict, again the risk of a lost job, which goes against the resolution of the 'problem to solve' which we identified: being promoted. In light of this context, knowing that she is intelligent, the rational strategy developed by the shampoo girl is understandable: do not offer products to customers; this is her strategy regardless of her desire to make more money. This is the bounded rationality of the actors; this is what must be understood, 'listened to' as we have said, if we want to have some chance of glimpsing the reality behind organizations, and therefore to change their functioning, which, as we saw in Part I is now so very necessary.

It should also be added that even though we have analysed a rather simple setting – the beauty salon – with what we might call a sophisticated concept – bounded rationality – not at all new in the sciences, this concept stands largely misunderstood, victim of the dream of a 'best solution' which the actors could find if only they were provided with adequate information. This is the illusion which Alan Ehrenhalt exposes when he writes:[10]

> Modern economists probably know more than astronomers in the Middle Ages, but they are themselves prisoners of a simple idea which dominates their thinking: most people in daily life are rational people who carefully calculate what is in their own best interest. They are, in economic jargon, 'maximizers of utility'. If they are given sufficient information, they succeed every time in coming to a logically correct decision.

The idea of maximization of profit is not the problem. This was explained in clear terms by authors such as Albert Hirschman, Raymond Boudon and even, surprisingly, by Tocqueville.[11] There is a logical flaw in the idea of a 'logically correct decision' which goes back again to the old notion of 'one best way', of 'the sharpest needle' and so on. From this standpoint, it would be possible to make the actors predictable – which is the fantasy of every manager who wishes to implement change – simply by giving them the information which would allow them to be 'reasonable'.

'What I have just said could be understood by schoolchildren', said the president of a large French company undergoing some hard times, having lost almost all hope in the face of fierce opposition to his rescue plan on the part of unions and even salaried employees. In fact, he saw that although even when provided with frank, honest, accurate information, actors were still unreasonable, at least from his point of view. Bounded rationality therefore does not imply that the actors are right, nor that they should be told they are right. It is not about giving permission. It expresses the calculations (in the sense of choices) which people make so as to solve one or several problems, the most urgent ones, based on an evaluation of their resources and their constraints. Even if this short definition seems to rule out the perfect predictability of an actor's behaviour – at the most, we might be able to say something about how consistent an actor's behaviour may be – we will see later on that it opens nonetheless some interesting pathways in dealing with the management of change.

How to identify the relevant actors

Let us now turn to a pedagogical exercise which consists in going back to the different concepts used to analyse the so-called case of the 'shampoo girl', explaining them one by one. By explaining we do not mean just coming up with 'tricks' or techniques – we will still be relatively powerless before the two-dimensional paradox of human behaviour: unpredictable and yet intelligent. Rather, it means shedding light, step by step, on a mode of reasoning which makes a little more cognizable the organizational complexity which this book has emphasized over and over again. How this is done will be presented with a grid, a tool which should help readers actually put into practice this new way of reasoning, applicable to any human system for which one can put together enough relevant information. The grid looks like this:

Actors	Problems to solve	Resources	Constraints	Strategies

There is nothing mathematical about this tool. There is no recipe which guarantees that such a grid can be filled in without error. There is no scientific proof for a correct solution. But a discussion of these five basic concepts – to which we will later add two more, power and uncertainty – will enable us to reason in terms of the entire collective unit, and to construct a methodology for conducting change.

Every attempt at understanding organizational reality – whether concerning the relationship between actors, or the strategy developed by one of them – assumes that all relevant actors can be identified, that is, those who must be taken into account if we want a reliable interpretation of the phenomena in question. Of course, here 'actor' is not the same thing as 'individual'. An actor frequently has a collective dimension (flight attendants, customers and so on). Furthermore, relevancy does not mean one's direct and visible involvement in the problem. We saw this in the case of the beauty salon, where our attempts to understand why refusing to offer products to customers was a rational strategy for shampooers led to the discovery of actors above and beyond the two directly involved (the apprentice and the customer): namely, the owner of the salon and the technicians, who are part of relevant context of the relationship.

Note once again that the concept of an actor, once it is well understood, facilitates the use of systemic reasoning, beyond a linear, causal or structural vision. More specifically, the actor concept allows us to see that problems are more concrete than structures: to analyse the functioning of a structure usually gives a rather poor result. Actors within a structure are not necessarily connected, and in daily life, are typically not concerned with the same questions. On the other hand, to start with the problem (in the case the symptom) one can identify rather quickly which actors are directly or indirectly involved, regardless of the official structure of which they are a part.

A quick illustration of this: a beverage company, with a high sales volume, complains of trouble in the purchasing department and embarks on an investigation to help it make some crucial decisions. The study involves conducting interviews which, understandably, the company suggests should take place within the purchasing department, in particular with the department manager, the product managers and the purchasers. Here, the relevancy of the actors is likened – reduced, one might say – to the structure of which they are a part, the one which is thought to be the cause of the problem. Supposing now that we ask those in charge to express in concrete terms what they see as the principal problem. They explain in no uncertain terms that they are not able to convince their purchasers to avoid overstocking packaging materials, in other words, to limit their purchases to the immediate needs of production.

Let us say, then, that there is one main problem, the purchasing of packaging materials, and that around this problem a certain number of actors interact, regardless of the particular structure of which they are part: the purchasers of course, but also the production manager who is the one most bothered by the problem of surplus inventory. These two actors are part of the company, but work in different departments. Furthermore, how could we understand what is going on if we do not take into account the suppliers, who, moreover, are non-members of the company, and *a fortiori* of the purchasing department? They are, by definition, key actors. In short, around the problem in question there is a network of actors whose connections form what is called a system, provided that these connections are more or less stable. Obviously, if purchasers' job performance is evaluated on the unit price of the item purchased, their shared interests with outside suppliers will be stronger than with the production managers in their own company. Two conclusions can be drawn from this simple example: the first is that in such a context, without any doubt the purchase of huge quantities of bottles is for the buyers a rational strategy, in the sense that this expression was given earlier in this chapter; the second is that once again in understanding organizations, the concept of a system is much more useful than the knowledge of structures which, like everything related to rules and procedures, is relatively abstract with respect to the real behaviour of the actors.

Finally, note that in an attempt to cast some light on organizational reality, identifying the relevant actors does not necessarily happen in one fell swoop. It is the result of careful reflection. This was illustrated in Chapter 1, in the analysis of the public system of ground transport carriers in France, where only at the end of a lengthy analysis did we happen upon the insurance companies as the key actor in the system, permitting the externalization of costs on to all motorists.

The concept of a 'problem to solve' is central to strategic and systemic reasoning. Let us recall why: the actors are rational not with respect to a general, abstract, scientific or ethical model, but with respect to what they have set concretely as their own goals. As was said earlier, one can only modify an actor's behaviour – or at least control this attempt at modification – if the rationality of the behaviour (and thus, the problem to be solved) has been understood. Why? No doubt because the 'problem to solve' is the key concept, as well as the most difficult one. Once again, there is no recipe to come up with the 'right' answer; no 'strings' which guarantee a correct interpretation; only the necessity of listening to the actors in the true sense of the term, and with this listening to develop a hypothesis, continually questioning, continually verifying what they are trying to achieve.

'Listening', a critical and hazardous exercise

There are three reasons why this exercise is particularly tricky and uncertain. In explaining them, we will be able to say a little more about 'listening', before taking the concept even further in the following chapter.

The mayor, the jobs and the land

Above it was said that a system is a network of interdependencies among actors, related around a single question. The first difficulty lies in the obvious fact that it would be somewhat naïve to jump from the idea that these actors are all concerned by the same question, to the idea that they all have the same problems to be solved, which might be, for example, the resolution of the question. A quick example serves to illustrate this point.[12]

In the 1970s, a labour conflict arose in France, typical in its day, concerning joint worker–management control. The company in question was called Titan Coder, a truck trailer manufacturer. Government officials in charge of business matters of the day, absorbed in eliminating 'lame ducks', decided that there was no way a French trailer manufacturer could make money in a tight market, and tried to interest foreign investors (primarily Americans) to take over the struggling company. The conflict which ensued quickly became an issue of national concern, and employees took over the three manufacturing plants (Maubeuge, Marseilles and Chalon-sur-Saône), deciding to produce and sell trailers themselves. Everyone got involved, just as what happened around the closure of the famous French watchmaker Lip:[13] the prefects, the sub-prefects, local and national elected officials, chambers of commerce, unions and employers' associations, government ministries and so on, to such an extent that when we used this case study in the classroom, students would come up with at least 20 relevant actors. Students were invariably astonished by the actions taken by the mayor of Marseilles of the day, going so far as to call him stupid, saying that the mayor was incessantly suggesting a replacement solution which would allow saving 300 jobs at risk, even though they would be sent to another town. Asked why they felt this strategy to be somehow 'irrational',[14] the students would point out that a mayor always tries to save jobs in the area for which he or she is responsible. Yes of course, no doubt, in most cases: but that is an *a priori* model, and just like every model, it dismisses anything incongruous or incomprehensible which cannot be made to fit.

Here the error lies in identifying the problem to be solved: upon closer inspection, it becomes pretty clear that the mayor in question wanted to recover some well-situated pieces of land in his own district currently occupied by the manufacturer. This being the case, he was not really worried about the possible loss of jobs, it was not the main issue, even if, like everyone else, he made quite a fuss about it. It was a resource, an opportunity. Getting ahead of ourselves a little bit here, we could say that in this case the mayor's problem to be solved is the recovery of the lands, his resource the threat over jobs, his constraint that he cannot by himself evict the manufacturer, and that his strategy is to suggest that it go somewhere else: no value judgement, no ethical or ideological considerations here. We have done a simple 'reading' of reality, which, once again, is subject to error. Let us add that this mayor acts no differently from those around him. To put it bluntly, we could say that saving 300 jobs is the problem to be solved only by the 300 people whose jobs are at risk.

All the other actors, beyond the question which concerns them all and which everyone is making a fuss about, are dealing with their own particular problems, for this is how human organizations work – there's no point in taking offence. Moreover this shows that the key problem of management is not obtaining some abstract consensus on the general values which people adhere to, especially if these values do not interfere too much with their daily lives. Rather, it is understanding the whole set of strategies, and then finding the levers by which they can be made to move in the direction which leaders intend, since this is their job as leaders. We will return to this point later on, when stressing that if an organization can be understood as a set of 'rational strategies', to change this same organization implies changing actor's strategies.

Frequency of meetings

A second difficulty has to do with the fact that identifying actors' problems does not mean that they are themselves conscious of those problems. It is a simple truth that you do not have to know what you want in order to want it, and that even without knowing it, you can still obtain it. This assertion brings us back to the problem of listening mentioned above. To 'listen to' the actors is not to ask them what they want and then to act receptive and listen to what they have to say. Typically, the actors do not know what they want, and the very question will only give them a guilt complex about it. To illustrate this point, whenever a leader says to a subordinate 'you do not know what you want', the latter could very well respond by saying that it is the leaders' job to know what their subordinates want. That is listening, and once again, its interpretive nature must be emphasized. To sum up, listening takes what one individual has to say about reality, and compares it to what others have to say about the same reality, so as to form a hypothesis on what the actor – once again, an individual or group of individuals – is trying to solve.

Let us take as an illustration the following classic experiment which anyone might try. Take two individuals A and B within any organization, knowing that A is the hierarchical superior of B, and ask them a simple, clear, precise question. In theory, we should not question the answers to this question, once we have made the mistake of believing that the actors 'should' tell the truth. We will see that they do not tell the truth, but not because they are lying – as soon as we start thinking in terms of truth or lie, good or evil, we are no longer 'listening' to anyone – but because there is no truth, or at least, its existence is far removed and abstract with respect to everyday life. Actors, when interviewed or simply spoken with, do not tell the truth, they express their way of seeing reality, or the perception which they think they should communicate to their environment.

The question which we are going to ask two particular actors is how frequently they meet in the context of their job. Say that Mr A states unhesitatingly that he meets with Mr B four times a month, and that Mr B with no more hesitation reckons that they meet five times a week. Must we conclude that one of the two is lying? Of course not. Instead, we should use this discrepancy in their perception of the same reality to help us see that for Mr B, their relationship is more important than it is for Mr A. The question is then: what problem does Mr B seek to solve since he has such a high, or perhaps overly high opinion of his relationship with his boss? Let us consider one response of a hundred possible, and suppose that this example takes place in one of the classic bureaucracies which is the very subject of this book. B is himself a mid-level executive who is in charge of a certain number of subordinates (call them C, D, E, F and so on). These employees cannot deal directly with boss A, insofar as they have to follow the overall hierarchy of the organization. On the other hand, in a bureaucracy where everything is governed by rules and procedures, B has very little control over his own employees. He does not grade them, review them, promote them, decide when they can take their vacation and so on. The only way he can get something from them is to assert each morning that he just met with the boss, and that he learned something important for everyone, without ever saying what it is about. To introduce a concept which will be elaborated later on, he creates uncertainty. What simple truths have we learned? That Mr B's problem to be solved is controlling his subordinates. Does he know this? It is of no consequence. And the strategy which he uses to secure control is at once to monopolize on access to the boss, and to underscore or even exaggerate how often they meet.

How is this kind of analysis useful, even in such a simple case, in everyday life? Say that a new Mr A is appointed, who has no advance knowledge about the organization he is joining, but equipped with solid principles – models – which he learned in the very best business schools. When in charge of an organization, leaders must, he has been taught, open their door to everyone. Once involved in his new job, he does not ponder the problem, but applies solutions, which are going to prove his worth. Summoning C, D, E and F into his office, he tells them how he hopes to have a direct relationship with them and that his door will always be open if they would like to talk. The employees, who see no harm in the situation, begin to speak openly with their boss with whom previously they had no contact. A little while later, what do we observe? Mr B is withdrawn, he ceases to involve himself in his work, no longer participating in the group as a whole. And Mr A will be able to say that his excellent education allowed him to diagnose the situation of his new organization in less than two weeks: mid-level executives (Mr B here) have no motivation!

Of course this conclusion misses the mark. Mr A has not really understood anything, and because he applied a model *a priori*, without investing in knowledge, he has not learned to control the effects of his decisions, which, even on the micro-social scale of this case study, produced the wrong results.

Let us go back to the beginning, using the proposed grid: Mr B, 'low-level leader' of a bureaucracy, seeks to control his handful of subordinates. This is his problem to be solved. He has a powerful resource which is his monopoly on access to the 'high-level leader', and his principal constraint is his lack of real power over the members of the organization. His strategy, as we said, is to preserve his monopoly. From the outside, one might be led to say that he is 'not very open', that he 'keeps tight control', and so on. In fact, he has a rational strategy which consists in preserving and using his main resource. When the new Mr A decides to establish a more direct relationship with his employees, he is applying an abstract principle, and the only concrete result on the existing system is to eliminate Mr B's only way of staying in the game, say his only resource. And what is the rational strategy of an actor who is out of resources? It is to withdraw from the game because the actor is intelligent, and not as a consequence of some theoretical lack of motivation. Here again, real discussion of the problems which actors have to be solved opens new doors to managing change.

The dispatcher and the delay

The third difficulty which we mentioned deserves a rather lengthy digression, for it allows us to tackle the problem of uncertainty and power in organizations.[15] Whether the actors are or are not aware of their own problems to be solved, it is rarely in their interest to say so, to put it in full view, unless they can be absolutely sure that it will not lock them into a situation of dependence.

And indeed, in any human system, as soon as actors know what is important for one of their group – what that particular actor seeks to do – they can assess in what ways they control that actor – the uncertainties – and thus the power which they derive from them, that is to say, in short, their ability to negotiate with this actor from a position of strength.

To illustrate this crucial point, which will take us back to the conditions for co-operation mentioned in Part I, we will use an example from the air transportation industry, which for reasons of clarity, we will modify somewhat. One need not be a specialist in the business to know that, on one hand, the less time planes spend on the ground and how on time they are on the other, are two conditions for the profitability of any airline. In particular, the so-called 'hub' system makes it especially important to minimize late arrivals, otherwise passengers will miss their connections, and the company will have to absorb any associated costs. Let us consider a large European company, a key carrier on the continent – let us call it X Air – which has established its hub at the principal airport in the country of origin. For X Air, as for the others, and especially given the climate of stiff competition which exists throughout the industry, on-time flights are a crucial factor around which the company tries to get all actors to work. And yet it is not easy to get a flight off on time, since preparing the aircraft, especially for long-distance flights, requires a whole set of complex operations. Even if we oversimplify, there are at least 11 important tasks to be accomplished, 11 specialized trade associations working simultaneously around the aircraft, so that it can take off at the scheduled moment.

Indeed, integrating these different activities is the key. On-time departure depends upon it, but such integration is very hard to achieve since the way X Air divides up its specialists means that each team working on the plane belongs to a different department or division, each under a different leader. The maintenance crew has little in common with the freight crew, and even less with the food-service crew. In the traditional organization of the company, one actor has been set up to ensure the co-ordination of all of these activities – we discussed the term earlier on – the co-ordinator. We have all had the chance to see a co-ordinator of this kind in operation, the last person to rush into the flight cabin, papers in hand, confirming that all is ready and that it is now up to the pilot to decide when to get under way. In the past, everyone agreed that X Air's co-ordinators did their job well, getting all of the different parts to work together well, which put the company among the top 10 airlines for on-time flight statistics! Concerning this harmony, many had emotional, even mythical interpretations: it is aviation, it is about reaching for one's dreams – manners were sometimes rough, but they were to the point, and in everyone's best interest.

Several years ago, in the face of growing difficulties, X Air reorganized, in the traditional sense of the term, that is, it changed structures, and tried to adopt the classic organization of a profitable modern airline. Suddenly, following the reorganization, activity around the aircraft deteriorated, fewer and fewer flights were on time, and co-operation gave way to conflict and complaints. When questioned, the consultants who were in charge of setting up the new organizational chart emphasize that they did nothing to change the situation. In particular, they note, with good reason, that previously co-ordinators had no hierarchical power to get the different teams to co-operate; the current situation is no different. They add that the current situation is probably either more tense, goodwill more difficult to find, or perhaps the co-ordinators themselves are younger and less hardened against people who are not easy to handle. In short, their interpretation of the concrete and radical changes which took place speaks about personnel and individuals, but not systems, and would clearly leave any person in charge both confused and powerless. This is why the question must be asked in a different way, in more concrete and practical terms. What was there in the previous situation that made co-operation with the co-ordinator a rational strategy for the members of the different teams working around the aircraft? Or, in other words using the concepts which were just introduced: what kinds of uncertainty did the co-ordinators previously wield over these teams to get them to co-operate?

This way of asking the question leads to another form of investigation, of pursuing the facts. It avoids concentrating on structures, definitions of functions and so on, and focuses attention on contextual elements, perhaps commonplace and unimportant in appearance, but which can turn out to be the very ones around which the system is structured. In short, it leads us to curiosity, to listening, in a situation that is unclear, that is, without turning to interpretive models which do not belong to the specific reality which we are trying to understand.

Here, let us add straightaway that co-ordinators, in addition to their integrational task, are responsible for assigning, when the aircraft is ready to go, what is called the 'late code'. This means that if, after all, the plane does not leave on schedule, it is the co-ordinator's job to determine and indicate who is responsible. This is all we need to know to see that they control uncertainty which is all the greater since there are so many complex, interwoven causes that can make a plane late, among which co-ordinators, in the end, can choose as they please.

The analysis does not end there, however: uncertainty controlled by an actor only gives that actor power if it is relevant, that is, important in respect to a problem which one or several other actors, or the organization itself is trying to solve. The notion of relevancy helps us understand why it is hardly in the actors' best interest to reveal themselves: 'Tell me what you want, and I'll know if I've got you under my control!' In this instance, the assignment of the late code is a relevant uncertainty not only because the remuneration of the different crews can depend partly upon it, but because their autonomy depends upon it. Remember that the quest for autonomy is often a crucial problem to be solved within organizations. A single example of this is that so long as the maintenance crew is not responsible for late departures, their boss will leave them relatively free to do their work as they see fit, to choose their own teams, to schedule their own breaks and so on. As soon as their team bears the responsibility for late planes, bosses are forced to 'intervene' to prevent a bad situation from getting any worse.

The power of the co-ordinator therefore has nothing to do with the official hierarchy. It can often be even stronger than what has been described here. If, for instance, there is a late departure, but all members still seem to have done their job, the co-ordinator is the only person who can negotiate on their behalf so that no penalty is assigned. The last ones to enter the cockpit, co-ordinators can always ask pilots to accept the late code, since they are never penalized, on account of their absolute freedom to decide whether or not the plane is ready to take off.

What happened then during the 'reorganization' which might explain the abrupt change in the behaviour of employees and the sudden increase in late departures? As is often the case, it was the result of good intentions based on principle, but without knowledge of reality. The organizers believed that, given the important role of the co-ordinators with respect to on-time departures, it was useless, even absurd, to ask them also to carry out bureaucratic tasks, such as the assignment of the late code. This was therefore taken away from their job responsibilities, so as to leave them more time to devote to work 'on the job'. But, in terms of concrete consequences, this was to take away the only real power they had, and for this reason made it much less rational for the different teams to co-operate with them.

What consequences might this have for the development of a frame of reference, as well as for managing change? Organization is not structure. We said it in Chapter 1, and confirm it here, seeing at the same time that power is not hierarchy. But if both statements are true, changing an organization is not changing structure – as we saw – nor 'positioning' certain actors within the hierarchy so that they have more power. Much more profoundly, it is changing the real distribution of this power, giving to the pivotal actors real, practical levers which they can use, which have a bearing on the reality of the problems which the actors we want to see co-operate are themselves trying to solve. Co-operation, once again, is not about goodwill or common sense. It is or is not a rational strategy for the members of the organization. It cannot be decreed; it is built up. A few examples of this are provided in the following chapter.

The leverages for change

From this point on, understanding the concepts of resources and constraints is easy. A resource is what an actor can put to use in the resolution of a problem; a constraint is what must be confronted. The result is that for actors, resources or constraints are never abstract: they exist only in relation to what they (the actors) wish to obtain. Here again there is no ready-made model; emphasis is on the unknown, and thus on listening. For one aspect of the picture which, at a given moment, is a resource, can become a constraint, and vice versa. It all depends on the problems which the different actors are trying to solve, and around which relationships are built. Note that this ability to change constraints into resources is precisely what is called, in a traditional approach to business, opportunity management. There is a classic example of this used to explain the notion to young students: let us say there is an organization in which a rule states that work begins at 8:00 am. To ask whether for employee Y this rule is a resource or a constraint is abstract, so long as one has not yet identified the problem which Y or Y's boss – for simplicity's sake – wishes to solve. If, on Monday morning Y would prefer to come in at 11:00 am because of some personal matter, then the rule in question is a constraint. It will require Y to negotiate with the boss's goodwill. But if on Tuesday, the boss asks Y to come in on Wednesday at 6:00 am to deal with an emergency situation, then this same rule can be a resource.

This example is not trivial, for it takes us back to two of the main themes: on one hand, the nature of rules and procedures within an organization, and the nature of management on the other. As for the first theme, we see that rules and procedures do not define what employees do. They use them both as resources and constraints, make them their own, and in the sociological sense, play with them.

This is nothing new:[16] formal structures, written or customary rules – culture, one might say – form the context of the actors, to which they adjust with the intelligence which we believe them to have. But we can go further here: the intelligent adjustment which actors make, suggested here, not only affects their strategy (the context having been changed, I adapt my strategy) but also the problem to be solved, which in the end opens up many new possibilities for managing change. The order in which this argument has been presented here – actors, problem to be solved, resources, constraints and strategy, was chosen for the demonstration. It does not necessarily reflect the line of thinking of actors whose intelligence leads them naturally to give top priority to means rather than ends. More bluntly, they focus on possible goals, those which they think they can achieve in the context in which they find themselves. The result is that one modification of this context can lead these actors to change priorities, to focus on new problems, and afterwards, and only afterwards, to adapt their strategy to them.

A simple example: participants from all over the United States have come to attend a week-long seminar on the Bloomington campus of Indiana University. Having come by plane and then by limousine, they are left with no personal means of transportation. For their first evening off, this 'constraint' will lead them, as the problem to be solved, to focus on spending the best possible evening in Bloomington. Now suppose that a professor announces, near the end of the afternoon session, his intention of going to Indianapolis for dinner or to attend an evening football or basketball game. A participant might now consider this professor to be a resource, and can focus on a new objective – spending the evening in Indianapolis – without even having to have decided what to do there. That can be determined upon arrival.

The problem demonstrated by this example clearly opens up a whole new set of possibilities for introducing change into organizations: the fact that intelligent actors in the end select their own goals out of what is possible, leads us to view certain contextual elements as levers which can be used in such a way that the actors will modify their priorities and strategies. Here we see why rules of human resource management, taken in the largest sense – salary, review criteria, promotions and so on – have tremendous potential concerning the transformation of organizations in general and bureaucracies in particular. Some commercial banks in America have understood this, setting as the number one criterion for employee review the ability to co-operate: rather surprising in a world where numbers are king! The banks measure this ability, for instance, as a function of the volume of business that customer representatives generate on behalf of their co-workers, or the number of customers they work with in conjunction with other members of the organization. In this case, co-operation is no more natural than in any other classic bureaucracy, but it becomes one of the strategies adapted by actors whose problems to be solved have been modified through the use of levers. From the all-important quest for autonomy, they have moved on to the necessity of co-operating so as to satisfy the criteria upon which they are reviewed.

Bringing this clarification of resources and constraints to a close, let it be said that the other actors must be included. Of course, this has nothing to do with our affection for them, even if we have the natural tendency to 'like' our allies and dislike those who are in a position to block our way. But in organizations, alliances and confrontations, just like other contextual elements, are frequently turned upside-down.

There remains the concept of strategy, which has already been developed to some extent. It can be defined, in short, as the rational calculation made by the actors to solve the problem which seems to them either most attainable or most urgent, after an evaluation of their resources and constraints. 'Calculation' is not used here in the sense of 'mathematical determination'. The actors very rarely sit down, head in hands, thinking through what to do. Such methods would cause them to err just as often as a more spontaneous method! Calculation is used to convey the freedom of the actors, never fully backed into a corner, always able to maintain all or some of their unpredictability, and who are continually making choices which translate into their strategy or strategies. The idea of choice in the day-to-day experience of management is always hard to accept because it implies the enormous responsibility of the choice-maker, who, of course, would rather claim that a decision is simply the 'only possible solution', and that, consequently, anyone would come to that same decision. This is not the case, and is why it is so difficult to run an organization, perhaps even in the end impossible, if we understand the expression in the voluntarist sense which it is often given. Organizations do not respond to a set of clear guidelines which actors would be willing to follow because they are fair, logical or reasonable. Organizations are the whole set of rational strategies which develop over time, one strategy in respect to another, and upon which each contextual modification has an influence, in a way which most often seems unpredictable or random, because we do not first bother investing in the knowledge of human systems. We do not have the time, and because we do not have the time we lose even more.

To those who wish to use the frame of reference which has just been presented, a final word of advice. Since reality is of such great complexity, I have suggested a grid with boxes to be filled in. It is reassuring to have something other than emptiness staring us in the face. But I have tried to emphasize that what is important is not the grid, which must not be reified as a tool which can always be trusted or which leaves little room for error. What is important, once more, is the line of reasoning. If this has been grasped, we might as well abandon the grid now; in using it, let us keep in mind these three principles:

1. It is perfectly legitimate to leave 'gaps' in the grid. These might indicate a lack of resources or few constraints on a given group or individual – the question mark alone is revealing. Gaps might also reveal our own lack of information or understanding.
2. The grid cannot be filled out 'bureaucratically' by starting with actor A, actor A's problem to solve, resources and so on – then actor B and so on. It works like a puzzle, piece by piece, by trial and error: it cannot be filled out all at once.
3. Above all, it is not an end, but a means: a means to understand the problem or problems at hand. In the example used to illustrate Chapter 1, that of the public system of ground transport carriers in France, the grid would have allowed us to see that fraud is a rational strategy for the helpless truck drivers, just as subcontracting out the most complex contracts is a rational strategy for those who are much less helpless. But the job does not end there. The problem is that these strategies arise because their cost is externalized on to the public as a whole through insurance companies. To move from the grid to the problem or problems: there is the process of listening.

Notes

1. For example, March (1981), March and Olsen (1976) and Allison (1971).
2. For an explanation of systemic analysis and its scientific foundations, see Crozier and Friedberg (1990).
3. This analysis, which will be presented in Chapter 7, comes from Roland Lussey (Bossard Consultants).
4. March and Simon (1958).
5. An extensive bibliography is presented in Friedberg (1993), pp. 387–405.
6. This study was conducted under the author's direction by Hélène Bovais, a member of Stratema Consulting.
7. The entire theory of motivation should be under the gun here, not only from a theoretical point of view (see Crozier and Friedberg, 1990) but from a practical point of view: since it represents a rather substantial approach to human behav-

iour in organizations, it regularly draws from models which are necessarily reductionist in respect both to the complexity of this behaviour, and the complexity of the organizations. Yet, taking into account – accepting – this complexity is one of the conditions for successful change. History has shown that the alternative is totalitarianism.

8. This is frequently the meaning given this term in France.

9. March and Simon (1958), p. 141.

10. Ehrenhalt (1997).

11. See Robert Reich's discussion of this in Reich (1992), pp. 23–4.

12. This case was studied by Dominique Thomas, working with the Association pour le Développement des Sciences Sociales Appliquées (ADSSA).

13. In the case of the French watchmaker Lip, workers besieged a closed factory and took over sales and production. The success of this early experiment in self-management was relatively short-lived.

14. It should be clear now that within organizations, there is no such thing as the 'irrational'. To suggest that an actor's behaviour is irrational simply reveals how difficult it is to piece back together the logic of his or her behaviour.

15. There is a superb discussion of the problems of uncertainty and of power in Michel Crozier's *The Bureaucratic Phenomenon* (1964). His example, the 'Industrial monopoly', which he uses again in *Actors and Systems* (Crozier and Friedberg, 1990), is today as valid as ever. It is unfortunate that some unenlightened minds who do not realize that examples retain their heuristic value with age, considering them 'too old' to be used for pedagogical purposes. Is the prisoner dilemma too old?

16. This is a recurrent theme in the sociology of organizations. For an in-depth discussion, see Friedberg (1993).

7

Listening to Bureaucrats and Changing Bureaucracy

Turning to the case study which will be used throughout this the last chapter, it is now time to go beyond the fundamental alliance which has structured the relationship between the leaders of bureaucracy on one hand and consultants whom we might call 'classic' – those who focus on process, structures, procedures – on the other. The first, most often outstanding, intelligent[1]... and sometimes cynical, are panic-stricken in the face of the sheer scale of their task. They do not see how they could succeed where so many others failed, faced as they are with motionless rank and file, fixated on its most recently won privileges and always ready to join in with the unions, which are also constructed around these bureaucracies and are well-adapted to their mode of functioning, their compartmentalization, their occupations. They realize that change is necessary, but, as we have seen, most often they view it from one of two angles:

■ through general, global plans which turn out to be so difficult to devise and put into practice that they never leave the drawing room – in which case people implicitly wait around for hard times to provide the window of opportunity for introducing change, and the human cost skyrockets;
■ or by attacking symptoms, selectively, usually through normative models, which it seemed in the past provided good results in specific cases (low productivity, increased failure rates, decrease in profit margins and so on).

Such approaches are manna in the desert for consultants, who have become true specialists of these 'best practices', and for whom, by definition, it is much more cost effective to work downstream rather than up, totally reconfiguring the process rather than first investing in knowledge of the problems. Such knowledge, as we saw earlier, can be quite humbling in that it brings new constraints into one's work (you must listen, ponder solutions, reject known, tried and true solutions) as well as lower profits: there are only a few things that one can in reality bring to organizations, and these are knowledge and implementation methodologies, help in defining a 'pathway of change' in unpredictable situations where we do not control what we might find or bring about; these often do not justify calling in planeloads of outside specialists, but rather require thankless, demanding, patient and long-term investment. In any case, it is a good bet that there is a source of a new form of information here, one that will be increasingly available as organizations face new constraints. In other words, the alliance mentioned above is the one created when we make the hasty jump from symptom to solution, allowing some to assert that they are interested in concrete matters, others to sell their 'products', and everyone to avoid dealing with the very problems which come in between (should come in between) the symptom and the solutions. It is in order to understand these problems that we must listen to bureaucrats and go back to the tools mentioned earlier.

Using a frame of reference, concepts, in order to listen may seem paradoxical. Indeed today, the notion of listening has become commonplace and has found its way into many 'unimaginative', generic approaches. The perspective is either that we must get closer to the customer because the market and our competitors require it, or we must pay attention to our employees in order to motivate them and hold on to the best of them. If this is the case, listening turns into either a by-product of marketing, or just one more incarnation of the modern methods of management, depending on where it is applied. It is also sometimes thought to be one of the intrinsic qualities of a leader,[2] in the same way for example as the ability to define and disseminate a 'vision'. From this angle, listening would be little more than a certain frame of mind, which could even be acquired if one could simply manage to convince people that is better to be open to others. Techniques used – in internal management, for example – include consultations and informal opinion surveys, or, on a larger scale, opinion polls and studies of company morale.

A strategic 'listening'

The sociological approach is altogether different. Strategic and systemic reasoning, as explained in the preceding chapter, allows us to go much further, asking questions in new terms, which are both not abstract, and extremely practical.

1. We have already shown[3] that listening can have organizational meaning when we try not only to know what the customer wants, but also to provide it. It was emphasized that the answer to the question, 'What is

an organization that listens?' is neither structural, functional nor procedural. One does not listen 'to the bottom from the top' by way of specialized divisions, but through modes of functioning. With a little humour, one might even ask, when the job of listening has been handed over *ad hoc* to some particular group within the organization, who is going to listen to the one who is listening, and how? The analysis of organizations has already said a great deal on this theme, although not always in the same words. The study of classic administrative bureaucracies for example, showed that the more an organization enjoys an absolute monopoly, the more the rationale of its internal functioning wins out over the rationale of its overall mission. In this case, there is very little listening to the environment, what there is is most often broken down into pieces, and what is learned is rarely shared with others. Likewise, we saw that an organization listens to its market more if its own members have an interest in doing so, in relation to what is at stake for them within the organization. They get both autonomy and power out of it, as will be confirmed by the example at the heart of this chapter.

2. Individually, listening is the application, in contact with others, either in one's work environment or elsewhere, of a mode of reasoning.[4] This mode comes about by understanding the words or behaviour of others in a way that is more analytic than normative or immediately instrumental. The problem is not about right or wrong, correctness or error; it is about being able to hear the reality which the actor who is speaking or acting is trying to convey. It therefore consists in taking into account the strategic dimension – in the sociological sense of course – of the words and behaviour of the actor.

In this sense, listening is an ability which can be acquired through strategic reasoning. As the result of listening, one does not simply repeat back to the actors, in a more or less paraphrastic or detailed manner, what they said: when this is done, they are disappointed and rightly feel as though they were not understood. Rather, the idea is, by comparing their words and their actions, to go from what these actors are expressing, their feelings, to an understanding of their reality, which from the outset has been called the organization.

To work with words – either through specific interviews or the daily exchanges which punctuate life at work – that is, to compare and place side by side different perceptions of the same reality, to interpret their strategic meaning, and from there to get at the system, is what is called here the 'listening process'. Furthermore, this process is built on an ability to control the mode of reasoning, and this ability should not belong only to the specialists, but should be part of the 'know-how' of management, enabling it to perceive what is concrete. For if this 'real reality' is not understood, not only is it hard to come to a good decision, but it is almost impossible to plan ahead, to control the effects of a given decision. Just as an engineer cannot rely simply on a given material's appearance to determine its electrical resistance, we need real knowledge of the systems that we would like to change so as to predict how they will react to these changes, especially when they reach the level of homoeostasis found in most bureaucracies.

The European Bank of Development: a twilight case

This process will be illustrated by an example which stands out for three reasons: first because the leaders have such a hard time understanding the functioning of the organizations in their charge; second, because there is considerable misunderstanding as a result; and finally because a 'virtual world' comes into existence, over which those in charge have very little control, which justifies them in their nervousness.

We will see that it is the identification of the problems that enables us to first feel out how much room we have to manœuvre in, to determine what levers we might be able to bring into play, and then to build words of change which are meaningful for the actors, since they are the result of real listening. The example presented here has been adapted so as to provide a clear illustration of how one might use the frame of reference which is being proposed.

The European Bank of Development (EBD) is losing both money and customers as the 1990s draw to a close. These are the symptoms which justify calling in outside consultants.[5] This bank was established in the late 1950s, and has a strong presence in southern Europe, especially in Spain, but also in Italy and Portugal. Corporate headquarters are located in Madrid and thanks to a very strong business network in this country as well as the systematic opening of branches, the EBD had quick success with individual customers: one million sales outlets are spread throughout its territory, even into the most remote corners of the country. On the business plane, the EBD is not in the least bit behind its competition: it specializes in a full range of financial products, suitable to all kinds of customers from the most modest to those with sizeable monetary holdings or real estate.

Taking a look at the formal organization, the apparent clarity is striking, as is a budgetary procedure which seems to have been perfected and is running smoothly. The Spanish network has a matrix-like structure, articulated around the following characteristics:

■ At the top, Management Network Spain (MNS) is equipped with all of the main functions needed to run the entire group efficiently: marketing, sales, logistics, human resources, finance and management control. The appointment of the heads of these different functions is the job of the MNS's director, who, in turn, answers to the chief executive officer of the bank, in charge of the different networks.

■ The Spanish network is divided into 10 Regional Divisions of Management (RDM), and at the head of each is a regional director linked hierarchically to the director of the MNS. Each region is itself structured on a model identical to that of the MNS: the same functions are represented, the heads named by the regional director, who is their hierarchical superior and therefore in charge of their assessment and review.

■ Regional Divisions of Management are themselves classically divided into Branch Management Groups (BMG), with on average 8 to 10 in each region. Each BMG is under the authority of a group director who is responsible for financial and personnel management of his territory as well as business growth in the branches.

■ As for the branches, their set-up is simple and rather unremarkable. They are generally comprised of about 10 people, including the branch manager, customer service representatives (CSRs) and tellers.

■ Customers have been structured into four groups, numbered from 1 to 4, Group 1 representing the most valued customers. Each of these groups is administered by a customer representative: the portfolios of customers belonging to Groups 3 and 4 are given to the younger representatives, and those of Groups 1 and 2 to the most experienced. It does not fall within the branch managers' purview to handle customer portfolios directly. Rather, according to their official job description, they are to provide support to the customer service representatives in selling products and services and, moreover, to contribute to the business growth of the branch, which is after all a rather vague turn of phrase.

Schematically, budgetary procedures are as follows: General Management of the EBD sets the main strategic orientation, especially concerning the volume of business. In reality, this orientation corresponds to what the Spanish network itself indicates as market potential, based on information gathered in the field. On this foundation, the MNS constructs a statement of intent, indicating for each region the expected results based on a certain number of criteria, such as levels of profitability and growth in the bank's net profit (BNP). Then, the procedure follows the hierarchical line, each level following the objectives set by the level above, according to the classic model of objective-based management (OBM). At the end of the line, Regional Management consolidates the estimates made by its colleagues and develops a regional budget which, again consolidated at the level of the MNS, is submitted for definitive approval by the General Management of the EBD. If, in the course of the year, there are significant differences between estimates and reality, it is the regional director's job to take the necessary measures.

For several years now, the EBD has been confronted in Spain with some rather significant difficulties: the bubble burst on some risky real-estate and financial investments made during some good years, and the press, both national and international, made quite a story of it, leaving the bank with the dreadful image of being under poor management. Moreover, the BNP has dropped year after year, unlike the bank's principal competitors, and customers, even those considered by the bank to be loyal, are slowly but surely turning away. It has been hard to stabilize profitability, despite every attempt to reduce costs and to improve productivity. This has led to a general decline in the social climate, revealed by ever-increasing misunderstanding between personnel who do not understand why nor how, despite their efforts, the situation continues to grow worse, and the leaders who continually tighten the screws on the customer service representatives, to get them to 'hold on to' the customers. As is always true in such a case, gossip is running rampant and unions have begun to push for better working conditions and job, career and salary security, in a world where methods of personnel management have been inherited from a more or less bureaucratic past, which, in any case, have no direct link with results.

Faced with these difficulties, the bank's leaders are at a loss: they see that there is a gap between the need for quick, serious action on one hand, and the behaviour of their co-workers on the other who do not seem to take the situation seriously, dragging their feet when asked to participate a programme of ambitious reform. These feelings are felt at every level in the hierarchy, each thinking the one below is protecting itself, taking the fewest necessary chances, and is hiding the truth concerning possible opportunities for business growth.

Verbatim

Let us now yield the floor to the different actors, highlighting the factors which enabled piecing together how the system was functioning,[6] or, in other words, understanding each actor's strategy, how each strategy is related to the others, and what it all means in terms of corporate performance.

Customers

Customers claim that the news media have kept them well-informed about the bank's problems. They bring the matter up with the CSRs, but admit that only a serious degradation in the bank's situation would cause them to take their business elsewhere. They are satisfied with the way they are treated, attributing this to the CSRs whom they view as distinct from the EBD, seen as a heavy, bureaucratic institution. Each customer speaks of 'his' or 'her' representative and enjoys the fact that their relationship is not strictly professional, often seeming more like a friendship:

> My customer service representative always calls when there is a new service which could be of interest to me. In all honesty, I'm happy to share my plans and concerns with him. Confidence goes both ways.

> I'm happy with the way they keep track of my accounts. The representative who helps me is always available and ready to find good solutions. I have often received discounts, such as on my spouse's credit card, or authorized overdraft.

There are of course some unsatisfied customers, but their dissatisfaction most often applies to the bank as a whole rather than their contact person:

> Last month, I was in quick need of credit. My representative closed the deal the very same day telling me that there would be no problem. But the bank's administration required more paperwork. He did everything he could but the two of us ran up against the sluggishness of the firm.

Finally, a very small minority of customers are very upset with the entire operation, either because they ran up against incompetent representatives, or because they were offered products regardless of their real needs.

Customer service representatives

In the interview, CSRs appear to be critical of the bank, satisfied with the way the branches function, and ill-at-ease in discussing their relationship with customers as well. The negative remarks about the company are typical, and are directed at all levels (the regions and network management). They concern the technocratic shortcomings of people who are out of touch with the real world, who come out with one plan after another, while making inadequate or even contradictory decisions; they emphasize deficiencies of the 'back office' and of the computer network.

> Since our troubles became public, we get the feeling that our leaders are in a panic. They are constantly coming out with new initiatives and plans to turn the company around, new administrative requirements, without even consulting one another, and so no-one has a clue what's going on.

> We must constantly take into account new instructions or products and for us this is just another bother, for none of it helps us work with our customers. There is so much going on that we can't possibly do everything, so we take our pick. In the end we feel like we are the only ones in this bank worried about the customers.

Concerning the branches, comments are much more positive, high-lighting both co-operation among personnel and the branch manager's key role.

> We get along, fortunately, since it is the only way we can stand firmly against the uncoordinated demands which rain down from above. The branch manager is really great. He helps us when we have a problem with the rest of the bank. And then he trusts us to work with customers.

> There are two important things in the branch: getting along and achieving our business objectives. We do our very best. If one of us is having trouble, we help out. For example, we can pass some of the objectives realized with our customers along to other representatives.

The relationship with customers appears to be more complicated. As in all organizations of this kind,[7] it is a source of satisfaction, but can at the same time create trouble:

> Customers are increasingly demanding and difficult, you cannot just sell them anything anymore. You have to be careful... Also, they know that their business is important to us, and with the bank's current troubles, they try to negotiate over everything.

Of prime importance is our autonomy within the company. We need it to build credibility with our customers, since they want to deal with just one person who can respond swiftly to their needs. This is why we avoid dealing with the hierarchy.

There are those who do what they can to sell 'everything and nothing' without charging the customer for services rendered. But this is counter-productive to the EBD's turnaround. But, so long as they sell products and customers are loyal, everyone looks the other way. Competition is tough in Spain.

Branch managers

The branch managers' clear-mindedness is nothing short of amazing: they have a good handle on their situation, fragile as it is, between CSRs who are fiercely protective of their autonomy and over whom they wield little power, and a hierarchy which, although rarely haggling with them, churns out one contradictory project or initiative after another.

Our hierarchy asks us to keep closer tabs on sales and profit margin. But the representatives do not want to hear this, since, as they say themselves, it threatens their autonomy in the workplace, and this goes against their customers' interests.

Our leaders must accept the idea that all of their grand ideas weaken the branches. But in my case, the regional hierarchy pretty much leaves me alone. As long as I meet the objectives, hold on to most of our customers and avoid any major problem in my own branch, I do as I please.

I'd be happy to do what our leaders our telling us, but we need to have the means to do it. How can the representatives hear what I have to say when they think that the customer is taboo, and cannot be shared, leaving me with no real way to assess their results? Their career future is determined somewhere else, and so no one knows if it depends on results or other considerations. What is more, now that there is no more growth, quick career changes are over, as the representatives know only too well. I would prefer to stay on their good side rather than fight with them. This is why I cannot be 100 per cent transparent in my dealings with the hierarchy.

Network management

Network management (the group director, the regional director and executives of the MNS) seems at a loss in the face of what it sees as employees' unwillingness to understand. It appears ready to thrown in the towel faced with the opaqueness of a system over which it admits it has no control.

> We have no real idea what goes on in the branches. When we meet with the managers and explain how bad the situation really is, they seem to want to give it their best. And then, once they are back at their branch office, they do nothing. If we want information, we always have to call them in.

> It is really difficult to challenge what branch managers have to say. If I tell them that I think they are exaggerating their problems, I must first be absolutely sure. But frankly, there's no way I can really know.

> We're faced with a kind of paradox. We have to change and to do this we need to know more clearly what goes on in branch offices. But, at the same time, they seem to close in on themselves, making it increasingly tempting to hide behind this opaqueness to avoid any big risks.

Breaking the vicious circle

These are the basic facts surrounding this complex situation. We see that outside the branch office, when co-workers should be helping one another, very little information is shared, and everyone blames everyone else for the bank's situation. The representatives have no faith in an unrealistic hierarchy which understands nothing, and which, at the highest levels, does not know whether to increase pressure to get the most out of customers or to inflict severe punishment on irresponsible employees who spend their time hiding the facts. In other words, it is an environment heavy with resentment, with thoughts unspoken, each group with its own interpretation of the shortcomings of others and of the system, and no one listens to anyone.

Let us break this vicious circle and, based on what has been presented, let us try to understand what is really going on. What we have to do is both to let the actors know that they are really being listened to – that their realities have been understood – and to let them come to their own realization of the problems facing the company, which should then facilitate searching for solutions as a group.

To do this, let us first look at the relationships between actors based on the interview data just presented. They are shown in Fig. 7.1, in which the + sign indicates a positive relationship, the – sign a negative relationship or one that is viewed as problematic, and the = sign stands for either a neutral relationship, one where very little is going on, or where there is no real relationship at all.

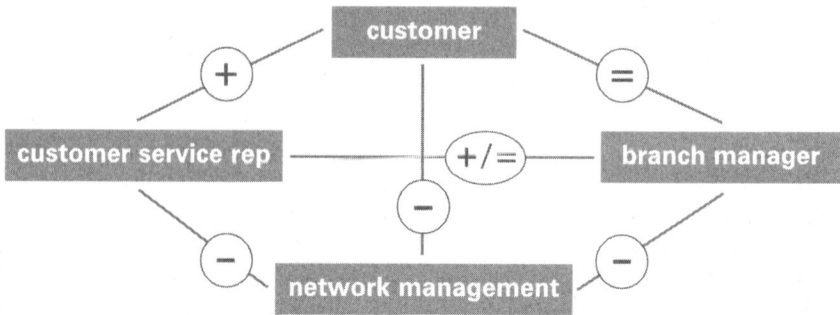

Figure 7.1   The relationships between actors

This little diagram highlights several key elements, paving the way for a more detailed analysis. The only robust relationship that is really positive is the one between the customer and the CSR. This is no surprise, for each side gets something out of the relationship: CSRs sell products and services by working with customers, while customers have their own representatives, who not only lend an ear, but even seem to understand their problems.

On the other hand, the remaining relationships are puzzling. Even though customers have no direct contact with network management (the BMG, RDM or MNS), they have a very bad opinion of them. No doubt such an opinion is useful to have when dealing with the CSRs. It allows them to underscore their great loyalty to the bank, which, according to the press suffers from poor management. It is a good argument for negotiation. At the same time, despite the apparent paradox, we see that representatives go along with customers in developing a negative opinion of their own bank. In so doing, they can emphasize their outstanding flexibility and adaptability within a paralytic, bureaucratic organization which offers them no help. In a way, we might go so far as to say that when a customer starts off by saying, 'You work in a bank which seems to be really poorly run', the representatives go even further, 'Oh well, it's even worse than you might suspect...'

In addition it can be seen that what has been labelled as 'network management' is rejected by all of the other actors: it is kept at a distance, criticized and condemned.

Last, the branch managers have a good relationship with the representatives so long as they do not intervene too much in their work and provide them with the resources they need.

A final remark to highlight the 'paradoxical co-operation' within the branch offices: here, results are exchanged whenever one of the members is in trouble so as to avoid any outside interference; however, customers are never shared.

Turning now to the analysis, it is clear that the key player is the CSR. They control a crucial resource – the relevant uncertainty in the system – that is, access to the customer, which is and will remain their monopoly, if they can help it. So long as they alone have access to this resource, shared with no one, not even with co-workers, not even *a fortiori* with branch leaders, they are free and autonomous. They organize their work and work schedules as they please, work at their own pace, and stay clear of supervision. They behave much like members of the liberal professions. To maintain this autonomy, which, as we saw earlier, is extremely important to the actors, especially in bureaucracies where there is little incentive to co-operate, the representatives have developed two strategies, which are not too difficult to identify:

1. They provide no information to the rest of the organization. As the only ones directly in touch with market realities, they cast *de facto* a shadow of total obscurity over the bank, in which it must try to survive.
2. To keep their customers, to win their loyalty and gratitude, to stand out from the rest of the organization, and – in their own minds – to save it from impending doom, they provide their customers with discounted or even free services, which have a negative effect on company profits.

Here we have a rather significant paradox of this organization, a rather surprising vicious circle: there is more and more pressure on CSRs to get close to customers thereby boosting turnover and profitability, but to do this, these very same CSRs offer them one benefit after another, making the bank's struggle for survival all the more difficult. The actors are all doing the best they can, each one develops a rational strategy, no one listens to anyone and everyone is mistaken. From a methodological perspective, two important points stand out:

1. The strategy of the actor considered central is easy to identify, if only because, in a general way, within organizations, strategies are clearer when the actors have more resources at their disposal;
2. This approach makes no attempt to 'cry scandal'. The representatives' behaviour is not 'scandalous', 'revolting' or 'irresponsible', to use just a few of the terms which the author heard as this work was being pieced together, and which only slow things down. Their behaviour is rational, that is to say linked to the context in which it develops, which leads us to think in terms of practical levers, rather than in terms of guilt, punishment or, on the more positive side, enthusiasm.

Do branch managers, those who are supposed to run the show – a bureaucratic euphemism, which actually means 'figure it out yourself' – really have the means to intervene in the functioning which we have just described? Of course not! As in most traditional bureaucracies, they are 'heads' (hierarchical vision), but control neither of the two elements which could be a source of real power: access to the customer, or the ability to review representatives (to promote them, set their salary – all things governed by long-standing rules over which they have no control). This explains why branch managers cannot distance themselves from these troops which are beyond their control. Contrary to a widely held psychological misconception, management requires a certain amount of distance which provides them with a measure of strength in the face of those who are to be managed. Branch managers, like every intelligent actor, adapt to the context in which they find themselves and become lobbyists for their employees *vis-à-vis* the rest of the organization. In this way, they contribute to overall opaqueness, protecting their colleagues, exaggerating their problems so as to receive more means, feeding inexorably the bureaucratic process of the allocation of means, a process which becomes very involved since those who manage it, confused and feeling that their information has no connection to real needs, hide behind procedures so as to avoid taking any risk.

More generally, the network's upper management is the victim both of this opaqueness, and of the autonomy at the organization's ground levels, although at the same time it contributes to and sustains these problems. The way it is compartmentalized, by product lines for example, gives greater freedom to those who, in the implementation of the increasing number of projects (as poorly adapted or integrated as they may be), must take it upon themselves to decide what they will or will not implement, knowing that no one can challenge this possibility which is in the end one of the reasons for the bank's survival. In short, fragmentation at the top heightens independence at the bottom, all the more so since, because of the overall opaqueness of the system, the top lacks the information required to decide what to do, and so 'covers' itself by churning out one plan, project or initiative after another, tossed out at will by various groups whenever they feel obligated to do so in order to keep their own division from being held responsible for the overall results.

Let us turn now to two questions which we should be able to answer armed with a clearer picture of the system, and which lead us from the symptoms to the problem.

1. Why, in this rather favourable context, do customers still leave the bank, albeit not all at once?
2. How, in spite of rather poor results, do employees still meet their objectives?

The observation that customers take advantage of this way of functioning is no doubt true, and it is clear that they enjoy their relationship with representatives who are always ready to fight on their behalf against their own organization. There are limitations to this game, however: it lasts only as long as the real needs of customers – whether they are expressed or not expressed – correspond to the range of products which their representatives are able to offer them. If this is not the case, either the customers will not be heard and will reluctantly go elsewhere, or they will be understood but the representatives themselves will send them over to the competition, at least for a specific product. In this way representatives can hold on to their monopoly of the customer within the organization: the relationship that is 'not strictly professional, but often seems more like a friendship', acquired over time, leads them to sacrifice potential earnings in favour of a customer's satisfaction. To sum up, in this bank, those who handle accounts sell products they know to customers they know. As a result, the bank loses both in profitability and in customers, especially those who are the most complex and thus the most profitable. The problem here is the overall opaqueness of the system, held in place by each component, solidified by the fact that it is not in the interest of those who have a monopoly of the customer to share the least bit of their knowledge with anyone else.

The realization of objectives follows the same line of reasoning. Let us get away for a moment from the formal process of budget proposals and observe what is really going on. Although the official path is 'top-down', each level echoing within its own units what it is told from the level above, in reality things occur differently: each unit, in order to provide the top with the information necessary to develop an overall budget, gathers data from those in touch with the real world. In the end, the CSRs are the ones with this living information and who use it, intelligently, to minimize their own risks. Underestimation becomes the rule and no one has the means to monitor the well-foundedness of the indications and predictions which are provided. In short, representatives set their own objectives and can therefore always meet them. In light of what we saw before (systemic vision), we see why there is no contradiction between one's ability to 'meet the budget' and the losses which affect the company as a whole.

The fact that this game exists has not kept the bank from developing an extremely sophisticated system of budgetary procedures, accounting and financial reporting, and management control. But this system moves within a vacuum, 'churning out' theoretical data and producing statistics which reflect a 'virtual' organization. In bureaucracies, the virtuality of the management system is the counterpart of the opaqueness of the real organization. That does not prevent people from pouring considerable human and financial resources into it, however.

The diabolical duo opaqueness–autonomy is therefore the real 'problem' of this organization, and both the loss of customers and low profits are the most obvious symptoms. None of the actors are corrupt, or ill-intentioned. There is no conspiracy to bring this bank to ruin. Each employee does his or her best, acting intelligently (in the sociological sense) to save what can be saved. The actors themselves are not in question here, but how their strategies interact. They are all rational in what they do, we have listened to them to understand this, but in the end nothing works in the bank.

Once the rationality of the system has been understood, there is no point in blaming the 'guilty' actors, in trying to get them to behave differently (their strategy is the sum result of their adjustments to the environment), or in providing them with 'good' models of management. Remember that bureaucrats who cover their actions, withhold information and strike deals to the detriment of common interests – as they do in this bank – usually have only come to the bureaucratic mode of functioning by default, for lack of an alternative. The only ones who might bear some of the blame in this situation are the leaders who allowed these systems to develop and no longer wish to listen, hiding their heads in fear.

We might contrast this situation with another large organization with over 16 000 salaried employees working at night in conditions which the company itself admits are very difficult. To make working conditions possible and acceptable, employees devised solutions ('when you're done, you leave', for example) quite unlike classic management models, and which consequently have progressively excluded the managerial staff.

When the company wanted to 'to take them in hand' again by reintegrating executive management into these solutions, it ran up against fierce opposition which it interpreted as a refusal to work, latitudinarianism and so on. It did not understand that for lack of a credible alternative, that is, taking into account the real problems of night work in this industry (redundancy, chronic alcoholism), and for lack of meaningful dialogue, the employees had hammered out a real world unlike the theoretical definition, and were not ready to give that up in the name of general abstract principles or scholarly theories of management.

The listening approach helps explain why it is difficult to change – as already seen – as well as the process which comes out of this difficulty.

Let us go back now to the Spanish bank. One might, to define a 'strategy of change' (the expression is presumptuous), use the same line of thinking as that which allowed us to see the problem. Systemic vision yields systemic change, this could be our guiding principle. It implies that we should first find the sensitive point or points at which the system can be made to change in a real way, and the lever or levers which can be used to act upon these sensitive points. No one says the task is easy. It requires that we spend more time reflecting on the situation than worrying about it, and that the actors themselves must always be part of the process. In our example, the critical point upon which everything else hinges is removing the system's opaqueness. There is no point in changing the information network, the budgetary procedure, or investing in a more sophisticated computer network, so long as we have no clearer view of reality. With this in mind, to establish a CSR review process whereby they are no longer evaluated on what they produce – which is not exactly known – but on their ability to co-operate with others, would be undoubtedly one good path to explore. Just as in other organizations, this co-operation might be measured, for example, by the volume of business which representatives send over to their colleagues, especially to the specialized branches of the bank, involved with more complex financial services. If the review process can be made to have a considerable bearing on salary, promotion and so on, it will make it more rational for these actors to be more open, to be more communicative. This is not going to change their attitude of mind, but their calculation. At the same time, if we allow the branch managers to implement these new criteria, we will be giving them new tools to use with those whom they are supposed to 'motivate', we will be giving them the means to achieve the distance that they need, we will be restabilizing the relationship. It is a good bet that, with this new resource, they will be able to give up their strategy based on more and more means. By working in this crucial 'construction site' and making use of the levers suggested here

– there are of course many others – we can, over an undetermined length of time, tackle three other sites as well: budgetary procedure, but again, despite its importance, the overall opaqueness must first be lifted; human resource management, that is, at once the selection of criteria for managing employees, as well as the selection of the employees who will administer these criteria; and last but not least, the mode of functioning at the top of the organization, where compartmentalization, as we saw, served to reinforce the drive for autonomy at lower levels. To do this, it is reasonable to expect that the more a need for co-operation is created at the base among the CSRs, the less they will stand for the verticalization of those who decide; this pressure will cause the leaders to change their own modes of co-operation.

Seven key points to be remembered

It is important here not to overemphasize the particular proposals made for this example. What is crucial is the methodology, the path which was followed and which can be summarized in the following seven points:

1. We began with the connections among actors in the system, and a schematic of these relationships provided a first clue as to how the system works. With careful interpretation, it brought our attention on to the key relationships, and thus on to the key questions which the analysis must try to answer.
2. The strategies of actors were then brought to light. This is where the frame of reference is really useful. We had to reason differently, in terms of bounded rationality, in order to understand the solutions which actors had developed. At the same time, as mentioned earlier, strategic reasoning takes the drama out of the actors' behaviour, which is a necessary condition for building dialogue around the why of change.
3. These strategies were not taken individually, but as a network, in systemic dimensions. This phase is essential because it prepares the way for work on a strategy of change (how to tackle the problems?) and on the levers which might be employed.
4. At this stage, we brought out the problems in all their complexity, and yet we were able to state them in clear, simple terms. This is where listening came in, for these problems constitute the actors' reality – not in the vague way which they themselves perceive it, but as they expect to be able to formulate these problems with the help of their leaders or other experts, a claim that experience bears out. Only when the identi-

fication of problems is a joint task, as information is being pieced together, during talks and so on, will there be consensus based on what is said and not on whether this or that person is to blame. Some authors call this phase 'empowerment'. Through it, all those involved – not just those in charge – can express their own feelings about the reality of their problems, and more importantly, about the possible solutions.

5. This is the phase where we begin to reason out the duo priority actions/levers. The expression priority actions is preferable to 'solutions', since the latter is already used in traditional managerial rhetoric and implies rapidity, the hope of some automatic mechanism between the identification of a problem and the sudden, almost miraculous appearance of a solution. This is not the case. The process requires group work and numerous trips back to the field. This is where one might discover what are often only micro-decisions, which lie on the fringe of what *a priori* does not seem to be very important, since we are so used to what is general, global or all-encompassing.

6. If, in the process, there is a good dose of faith in the actors themselves, in bureaucrats, it is because if we want them to give up bureaucratic solutions (recall from Part I that giving these up is costly, painful and unnatural), they themselves have to see the necessity of it and find their own ways to do it. It is up to them to 'do things differently', to discover alternatives, to 'think the unthinkable'. This cannot be achieved with a predetermined plan which defines in advance all the steps of change, including the expected results. An organization cannot be 'un-bureaucratized' by way of bureaucratic means, one cannot go beyond Taylor by using a Taylorian approach.

7. Finally, each strategy exists only through its implementation, and should therefore be carefully evaluated. On this subject, a final remark: if we are going to change bureaucracies, especially the most cumbersome of all, trial and error is probably not the best way to go about it. An organization will more readily accept the implementation of change if is easily swallowed, 'marginalized', unlikely to spread or generalize. It is better to think in terms of 'critical mass', which can help influence what is called the 'system of reference' of the organization, that is, the set of customs, practices and arrangements made, with little threat of upsetting the organization. Changing the system of reference clearly takes time, a lot of time, more time in any case than would be required by a simple recasting, however complete, of organizational charts, rules, procedures and functional descriptions.

Notes

1. In the French sense of the term, as defined in the preceding chapter.
2. Cf. Bennis and Nanus (1997).
3. See Chapter 2, the case of the British food service company.
4. Cf. Chapter 4.
5. The majority of large international consulting firms come to the rescue of this bank which spends huge sums of money in search of good advice. At first, our efforts were viewed as relatively insignificant, part of a so-called 'social' diagnosis. The work was conducted by a team under the guidance of Dominique Gatto (Bossard Consultants).
6. I will of course limit the presentation to excerpts of just a few interviews. In reality, 150 interviews were conducted, representing around 2000 pages of data. Concerning the methodology used, see Friedberg (1988), pp. 103–22.
7. This is truly a classic bureaucracy. Cf. Dupuy and Thoenig (1985).

Conclusion –
Towards New Organizations?

Throughout this book, a central theme has been that of the profound, sometimes abrupt, but almost always painful transformation of technical bureaucracies, constructed for the most part on Taylor's scientific organization of work model. Once again, this trend is not new. It is almost universal in scope, even if the problem takes on different forms according to the specific environments encountered in different nations. Countries differ less in the rigidity of their bureaucracies – and indeed, extreme rigidity is not always on one particular side of the Atlantic as is often thought – than in their ability to question them, whatever the social and human cost. We are dealing with a strong underlying movement which goes beyond private business or public administration.

In the largest sense, these are the days of accountability: everyone wants everyone else to account for their behaviour, to the great pleasure of the believers in a state governed by law… and lawyers![1] In puritanical countries, elected officials are being asked about their private lives; civil servants are being asked about their use of public funds; even athletes about their use of drugs; and of course customers want explanations from their providers. In this case, the fact that there is competition – one or more alternatives for the customer – gives considerable weight to their demands. Even though we did not spend as much time on this point as we might have, it is clear that the customer's victory is closely linked to globalization.

However, if one looks at the day-to-day routine, the daily workings of the revolution of organizations in which we are all swept up, overall trends are as usual less clear, movements are not linear nor perfectly observable, they are even sometimes contradictory. And if, in the long run, everything seems to be headed in one general direction, three trends would seem to stand out at present.

The disappearance, or rather the alteration, of the borders between organizations and their environment

First with their customers, companies renegotiate the creation of value, or, more specifically the portion of value which customers would create themselves. If we say that a company is a machine for creating value, then the outline of this machine begins to blur, even if, once again, organizational charts continue to create an illusion of clarity. This trend can be found in such diverse sectors of the economy as furniture manufacturing[2] or the hotel industry: to enable customers to 'construct' what their own stay at the hotel will be like, using the palette of choices placed at their disposal, has today become the key to quality service in the industry. Taking another very recent example, the so-called 'Swatch mobile', the small Mercedes, follows the same principle: automobile production leaves the confines of the manufacturing process and offers customers a palette of services, which revolve around the use of the vehicle, but which reveals a much broader underlying vision. It is then up to customers to determine what they want to buy, what they wish to produce themselves, and what they require of their provider. These new developments, still in the minority, lead to two remarks.

The first, already mentioned in this book, is that the same level of adaptability or flexibility cannot be attained if we do not change the way we do our work, and the kinds of activities that each employee is supposed to do at his or her job. Specialized technical divisions, which are often considered more vital than they really are, are smashed apart, even if elsewhere other forms of specialization are appearing, especially in computer technologies.

But, returning to our classic bureaucracies, job status, work schedules and diverse job benefits are thrown into disarray, which explains some of the fierce attempts at resistance, which cannot be dealt with by simply saying these are 'delay tactics' of the rearguard... Again, what is being described here from this particular angle is how the victorious customers make the most of their victory, just as producers made the most of theirs, just as quickly, during the preceding era. Again, the two keywords are 'vagueness' and 'co-operation'. Vagueness, because these new organizations must accept that the shape which they are taking is subject to very rapid change,[3] and even that at some point there will be no one anymore with a clear knowledge of what, at least on the fringes, is part of the company strictly speaking and what is not. Co-operation because one cannot attain such a high level of adaptability and flexibility in a system characterized by verticality, segmentation and traditional processes. In other words, ISO standards, a modern version of Taylorism, or a lack of confidence in employees' ability to act and to act together, will not make possible the level of quality sought here.

But it is also worth pointing out that the borders surrounding the producers themselves are changing. Here again, there is the problem of apportioning the creation of value. Through 'total facilities management', multi-service strategies, which although still in the minority, are increasingly present in the market, occupations are being radically redefined. One's 'occupation' is no longer food service, housekeeping and maintenance: it is the management of a building, of a place, with the whole set of activities linked to managing that place. The consequences of such a change are many and it is as yet difficult to imagine them all. Before mentioning a few of them, I wish to emphasize one particular point. Recourse to what we can call 'integrated outsourcing' follows the same general line of thinking presented throughout this book: people want to get more from their providers at a lower cost. 'More' signifies an improved integration concerning the ever-present problem, which everyone who has wanted to 'have something built', such as a house, knows well, the fact that trade associations are broken up into small specialized groups and it can be difficult getting them to work together (integration) on a daily basis at the work site, a problem which costs the customer in terms of quality and delay. The answer to this is to find a provider who will take charge and reduce the cost of the set of individual operations. This approach – which has now appeared among builders in response to customers' need for transversality in respect to a product (the house) made up of complex parts – today has been extended to a whole set of services which companies no longer wish to provide themselves, and which they no longer wish to administer through endless one-on-one meetings either.

The most important consequence of this movement is beyond a doubt a reduction in the number of providers, which translates into the disappearance of some of them, and the melding of others into larger units with no distinct outline, under the leadership of the principal provider, whose role is that of a 'co-ordinator'. The entire automobile industry today – and it is not alone – implements the double strategy of drastically reducing the number of suppliers and integrating them into larger units, which takes us back once again to the vagueness of borders and the evolution of occupations, of what a job requires an employee to do. Ford will reduce the number of its suppliers by 95 per cent before the year 2000 and some customers will go so far as to offer their providers some of the money which these newly organized relationships will allow them to save. The issue of sharing value is indeed central here. The keyword is integration, and can without a doubt be characterized by multi-service operations. It is precisely what complex customers want, sophisticated customers, one could call them, who are not necessarily institutional customers: airline passengers who do a lot of travelling, and buyers of the Swatch mobile alike demand this integration and a different way of organizing tasks and job occupations which would put them, the customers, at the heart, and not at the fringes, of the production of goods or services.

A world of the future, one might say, in which not only is there no more room for bureaucrats, but which will come about through the 'liberalization'[4] and the 'nomadism', so to speak, of jobs. We are no longer very far here from some of the introductory arguments of this book concerning the radical disappearance of work in its most traditional forms.

And yet, the 'Taylorian' choice still exists

While writing the final pages of this book, I was in the United States for a discussion panel – with a focus on the transformation of organizations – during which the CEO of a company specializing in consumer credit and debt consolidation with 800 agencies throughout the United States and Canada, made the following profession of faith: 'I am certainly one of the last staunch partisans of Taylorism.' His quite convincing explanation is worth outlining here. It stresses a statistical rather than individual knowledge of the customer; it advocates the development of simple products, using the most industrial methods possible as the only way to reduce cost; it stresses the need to divide customers up based on behaviour patterns, each category associated with a particular value of 'risk'. In other words, it goes back to all the key ingredients of mass production. Indeed, not only is mass production still around, but one of the options is to manage it through bureaucracy, around a dual problem: reduce risk, reduce cost and, consequently, reduce individual knowledge concerning the customer and the freedom of movement of the organization's members, especially by way of sophisticated computer technology. This is what Alvin Tofler, going back to the words of George Orwell, called 'trying to make one's employees electronic plebs'.[5]

Today, this option is gaining acceptance because it seems like an alternative to the enormous investment required to transform the modes of functioning of organizations. Here is a striking example: when executives at inter-company instructional seminars both in Europe and the United States are asked whether 'you have the feeling, in your organization, that more and more rules and procedures are being generated', the answer is by and large yes. It seems to me that this reveals two aspects of the problem.

On one hand, there is the hope that the routine segmentation of tasks might lead to a level of quality sufficient for the customer who is most worried about price, and thus who is ready to sacrifice other aspects of the product's delivery. For the company, both risk and investment are minimized. Why not? This is the strategy chosen by most retail banks – not all – because they do not know how else to administer the relationship with a customer in whom, fundamentally, they have no confidence.

On the other hand, there are consequences to hiring employees who are less and less qualified, one more solution used to reduce production costs. A drop in qualifications such as can be observed in medium-size airlines in America, brings about *de facto* reduced confidence (again!) in the ability of employees to handle problems independently of a carefully detailed company handbook. But it is also, quite paradoxically, a small business movement: in some of my courses taught in the United States, students wrote final papers in which they provide a bounty of examples of the organizations in which they work, quite often local restaurants. Over and over again they make the same astonishing observation: their organization has been thought out in minute detail: intervals between courses are carefully timed, menu lists are memorized; in short, these are environments in which nothing is left to chance or to individual initiative, everything is calculated with great care so that production can be carried out without the least bit of previous know-how or experience. Again, why not? Even if, in other respects, the failure rate for these small organizations is alarming, and if, when all is said and done, the only ones which survive are those which manage to introduce into this nicely oiled process some 'organizational personal touch'.

Organizations are beginning to differ in their product/customer strategies

Organizations differ in how much they invest in the changing demands of their customers. For there is no determinism. Those who remain in mass production are not condemned to bureaucratic Taylorism: in companies specializing in consumer credit, as in mail-order companies (the two are linked), there are exciting new attempts at harnessing computer technologies. Proletarianization is not intrinsically part of this. These technologies allow the customer sales representatives to instantaneously visualize not only a customer's profile and 'buying history', but also his or her physical appearance, which, in terms say of apparel, will permit without delay personalized, suitable advice. What is more, these salespeople have been given 'room in which to manœuvre', that is to say, the possibility – however limited – to give rebates, to offer a particular benefit and so on. Here, confidence has been rediscovered, and, for the moment, the results are excellent. We are not far here from the case of the American banks mentioned earlier which decided to review their executives on their ability to work together rather than on the amount of business which they generate, even if their actions should cause a decline in overall results.

Clearly, at least in the short run, nothing is written in stone. Leaders and organization members are sent home to rethink their vision for the future, their choices and especially their ability to have confidence in each other, which is the unavoidable condition for introducing processes of change within organizations, by alleviating the harshest aspects of crisis, of tragedy or of constantly renewed pressure. We saw that this confidence does not fall within the Taylorian tradition, nor obviously in the promotion of elite groups. It must therefore be built from the ground up, around the sharing of knowledge, around the ability of each and every one to participate in the game, which is an absolutely necessary condition if we want individuals to accept a little more confrontation, a little more co-operation. And if, in the end, customer pressure, their increased number of choices and their heightened maturity are responsible for leading members of organizations to draw closer to one another in the fullest sense, to listen to one another as defined here, then this victory will serve some real purpose.

Notes

1. Crozier (1984).
2. Normann and Ramirez (1993).
3. See for example the alliances created and uncreated in the chemical industry, the co-management of one production unit by two groups, and so on.
4. In the sense of the so-called 'liberal' professions.
5. Tofler (1991), p. 255.

References

Allison, G.T. (1971) *Essence of Decision: Explaining the Cuban Missile Crisis*, Little Brown, Boston.

Argyris, C. (1991) 'Teaching smart people how to learn. Every company faces a learning dilemma: the smartest people find it the hardest to learn', *Harvard Business Review*, May–June: 99–109.

Argyris, C. (1995) *Savoir pour agir: surmonter les obstacles à l'apprentissage organisationnel*, Interéditions, Paris.

Arnaud, P. (1997) 'Le pouvoir contesté des médecins', *Le Monde*, 25 February.

Beer, M., Eisenstadt, R. and Spector, B. (1990) 'Why change programs don't produce change', *Harvard Business Review*, November–December.

Beer, M., Eisenstadt, R. and Spector, B. (1992) 'Pourquoi les grandes entreprises réagissent lentement' *Harvard L'Expansion*, Spring, pp. 93–103.

Bennis, W. and Nanus, B. (1997) *Leaders: Strategies for Taking Charge*, 2nd edn, HarperCollins.

Bergmann, A. and Uwaminger, B. (1997) *Encadrement et comportement*, Editions ESKA, Paris.

Birnbaum, P. *et al.* (1978) *La classe dirigeante française*, PUF, Paris.

Bisaoui-Baron, A. (1978) 'Origine et avenir d'un rôle balzacien: l'employé aux morts'. In Carvici (ed.) *L'année balzacienne*, Garnier, Paris, pp. 63–74.

Burns, T. and Stalker, G.M. (1961) *The Management of Innovation*, Tavistock, London.

Castel, R. (1995) *Les métamorphoses de la question sociale: une chronique du salariat*, Fayard, Paris.

Chaponnière, J. (1997) 'Les leçons de la crise en Corée du Sud', *Le Monde*, 28 February.

Cohen, R. (1997) 'A somber France, racked by doubt', *International Herald Tribune*, 12 February.

Crozier, M. (1964) *The Bureaucratic Phenomenon*, University of Chicago Press.

Crozier, M. (1964) *Le phénomène bureaucratique*, Editions du Seuil, Paris.

Crozier, M. (1979) *On ne change pas la société par décret*, Grasset, Paris.

Crozier, M. (1984) *The Trouble with America: Why the System is Breaking Down*, University of California Press, Berkeley and Los Angeles.

Crozier, M. (1994) *L'enterprise à l'écoute*, Interéditions, Paris.

Crozier, M. (1995) *La crise de l'intelligence: Essai sur l'incapacité des élites à se réformer*, Interéditions, Paris.

Crozier, M. and Friedberg, E. (1977) *L'acteur et le système*, Editions du Seuil, Paris.

Crozier, M. and Friedberg, E. (1990) *Actors and Systems*, Chicago University Press.

Crozier, M. and Friedberg, E. (1994) 'Organizations and collective action: our contribution to organizational analysis'. In Bacharach, S.P., Gagliardi, P. and Mundell, B. (eds) *Research in the Sociology of Organizations*, JAI Press, Greenwich, CT, vol. XIII.

Crozier, M., Friedberg, E., Gremion, P., Gremion, C., Thoenig, J. and Worms, J. (1974) *Où va l'administration française?*, Editions d'Organisation, Paris.

De Bandt, J. (1997) 'Renault, un triste cas d'école', *Libération*, 12 March.

De Bandt, J. and de Bandt-Flouriol, F. (1996) *La descente aux enfers du travail, ou l'économie sens dessus-dessous*, ADST, Paris.

De Bandt, J., Dejours, C. and Dubar, C. (1995) *La France malade du travail*, Fayard, Paris.

Deschamps, P.M. (1995) 'Pourquoi tout changer quand tout va bien', *L'Expansion*, 496, 6–19 March.

Drancourt, M. (1997) 'Révolution chez les managers, *Sociétal*, no. 4, January.

Duhamel, A. (1993) *Les peurs françaises*, Flammarion, Paris.

Dupuy, F. (1990) 'The bureaucrat, the citizen and the sociologist'. In *French Politics and Society*, Harvard University Press, **8**(2): 4–12.

Dupuy, F. (1992) 'Personne, n'écoute', *Le Monde*, 16 July.

Dupuy, F. and Thoenig, J. (1979) 'Public transportation policy-making in France as an implementation problem', *Policy Sciences*, **11**: 1–18.

Dupuy, F. and Thoenig, J. (1983) *Sociologie de l'administration française*, Collection U. Armand Colin, Paris.

Dupuy, F. and Thoenig, J. (1985) *L'administration en miettes*, Fayard, Paris.

Dupuy, F. and Thoenig, J. (1986) *La loi du marché: étude sur les marchés de l'électroménager blanc en France, aux Etats-Unis et au Japon*, L'Harmattan, Paris.

Ehrenhalt, A. (1997) 'Keepers of the dismal faith. How economists outwit common sense', *New York Times*, 23 February.

Fayol, H. (1917) *Administration industrielle et générale*, Dunod et Pinot, Paris.

Financial Times (1995) 'Tough schedule for take-off', 16 January.

Fitoussi, J. and Rosanvallon, P. (1996) *Le nouvel âge des inégalités*, Le Seuil, Paris.

Forrester, V. (1996) *L'horreur économique*, Fayard, Paris.

Francfort, I., Osty, F. and Sainsaulieu, R. (1995) *Les mondes sociaux de l'enterprise*, Desclée de Brouwer, Paris.

Friedberg, E. (1988) 'L'analyse sociologique des organisations', POUR, les dossier pédagogique du formateur, L'Harmattan, Paris.

Friedberg, E. (1993) *Le pouvoir et la règle*, Editions du Seuil, Paris.

Garelli, S. (1997) 'Même la Suisse doit changer', *Le Monde*, 4 February.

Gave, F. (1996) 'Le modèle allemand est-il en crise?', Centre d'études et de recherches internationales – *FNSP*, no. 19, September.

Grémion, P. (1976) *Le pouvoir périphérique, bureaucrates et notables dans le système politique français*, Le Seuil, Paris.

Hammer, M. and Champy, J. (1993) *Le re-engineering: Réinventer l'entreprise pour une amélioration spectaculaire de ses performances,* Dunod, Paris.

Harnel, G. and Prahalad, C.K. (1994) *Competing for the Future*, Harvard Business School Press.

Hassenteufel, P. (1997) *Les médecins face à l'Etat: une comparaison européenne*, Presses de Sciences-Po, Paris.

Henriot, A. (1997) 'Quand la flexibilité modifie les comportements économiques', *Le Monde*, 4 March.

Hesselbeim, F., Goldsmith, M. and Beckhard, R. (eds) (1996) *The Leader of the Future: New Visions, Strategies and Practices for the Next Era*, Jossey-Bass, San Francisco.

Izraëlewicz, E. (1997a) 'Big, small, beautiful', *Le Monde Economie*, 11 February.

Izraëlewicz, E. (1997b) 'Ombres et réalités chinoises', *Le Monde Economie*, 25 February.

Izraëlewicz, E. (1997c) 'Où va le monde?', *Le Monde Economie*, 18 March.

Kagono *et al.* (1985) *Strategic versus Evolutionary Management: a U.S./Japan Comparison of Strategy and Organization*, North-Holland, New York.

Kanter, R.M. (1989) *When Giants Learn to Dance*, Unwin, London.

Kanter R.M. (1992) *L'entreprise en éveil*, Interéditions, Paris.

Kanter, R.M. *et al.* (1992) *The Challenge of Organizational Change: How Companies Experience It and Leaders Guide It*, The Free Press, New York.

Kapstein, E.B. (1997) 'Capital mobile, travailleurs immobiles', *Le Monde*, 4 March.

Karlsson, C. and Ahlström, P. (1996) 'The difficult path to lean product development', *Journal of Product Innovation Management*, 13(4): 283–95.

Lampiere, L. (1997) 'Etats-Unis: pourvu que ça dure…', *Libération*, 8–9 February.

Laroche, M. (1997) 'Insondable confiance', *Le Monde Economie*, 28 January.

Lawrence, P.R. and Lorsch, J.W. (1967) *Organisations and Environment*, Harvard Business School.

Lawrence, P.R. and Lorsch, J.W. (1986) *Adapter les structures de l'enterprise*, Editions d'Organisation, Paris.

Lebaube, A. (1997a) 'La flexibilité toujours recommencée', *Le Monde Emploi*, 19 February.

Lebaube, A. (1997b) 'Pratiques syndicales flexibles en Europe', *Le Monde Emploi*, 19 March.

Le Monde (1984) 'La sécurité de l'emploi est absolument indispensable au bon fonctionnement de l'Etat', interview with Professor Piquemaz, 8 March .

Le Monde (1997a) 5 February.

Le Monde (1997b) 'Volkswagen relance ses innovations sociales pour résoudre ses surcroîts de production', 6 March.

Le Monde (1997c) 'On continue à ne gouverner que dans l'urgence', interview with Jacques Chereque with Laetitia van Eeckhout, 12 March.

Le Monde Emploi (1997a) 'Les auxiliaires de l'Etat patron', 5 February.

Le Monde Emploi (1997b) 19 March.

L'Equipe (1996) 'Rougé: "On change une équipe qui gagne"', 19 July.

Leseman, F. (1988) *La politique social américaine*, Syros, Paris.

March, J.G. (1981) *Decisions and Organizations*, Blackwell, London.

Libération (1997a) 'La France en marge de la société en réseau', 7 February.

Libération (1997b) 'Duisbourg: Le coup de grâce de la réunification', 24 February.

March, J.G. and Olsen, J.P. (eds) (1976) *Ambiguity and Choice in Organizations*, Universitetsforlaget, Bergen.

March, J.G. and Simon, H.A. (1958) *Organizations*, Wiley, New York.

Marti, S. (1997) 'La foi de Davos', *Le Monde Economie*, 4 February.

Midler, C. (1993) *La voiture qui n'existait pas*, Interéditions, Paris, p. 244.

Milano, S. (1996) *Allemagne: la fin d'un modèle*, Aubier, Paris.

Mintzberg, H. (1982) *Structure et dynamique des organisations*, Editions d'Organisation, Paris.

Mintzberg, H. (1992) *Structure in Fives: Designing Effective Organisations*, Prentice-Hall.

Morin, E. and Naïr, S. (1997) *Une politique de civilisation*, Arléa, Paris.

Moulet, M. (1982) 'Modes d'échange et coûts de transaction: une approche comparative de la forme et du marché', *Sociologie du travail*, **4**: 484–90.

Nadler, D. *et al.* (1992) *Organizational Architecture: Designs for Changing Organizations*, Jossey-Bass, San Francisco.

Nadler, D. *et al.* (1995) *Discontinuous Change: Leading Organizational Transformation*, Jossey-Bass, San Francisco.

New York Times (1993) 'The 6.8% illusion', 8 August.

Normann, R. and Ramirez, R. (1993) 'From value chains to value constellation: designing interactive strategy', *Harvard Business Review*, July–August: 65–75.

Ocqueteau, F. and Thoenig, J. (1997) 'Mouvements sociaux et action publique: le transport routier de marchandises', *Sociologie du Travail*, **4**: 397–423.

Ohmae, K. (1996) *De l'Etat-nation aux Etats-régions*, Dunod, Paris.

Ouchi, W.G. (1977) 'Review of Williamson's *Markets and Hierarchies*', *Administrative Science Quarterly*, **22**: 541–4.

Parker, M. and Slaughter, J. (1988) 'Management by stress', *Technology Review*, October.

Quinn, R. (1996) *Deep Change: Discovering the Leader Within*, Jossey-Bass, San Francisco.

Reich, R.B. (1992) *The Work of Nations. Preparing Ourselves for 21st Century Capitalism*, First Vintage Books, New York.

Reynaud, D. (1989) *Les règles du jeu: l'action collective et la régulation sociale*, Armand Colin, Paris.

Rifkin, J. (1996) *The End of Work: The Decline in the Global Labor Force with the Dawn of Post Market Era*, Putnam Group.

Roethlisberger, F.J. and Dikson, W.J. (1939) *Management and the Worker*, Harvard University Press.

Rouze, J. (1993) 'Frederick K. Taylor, inventeur de la démocratie moderne?', *Gérer et Comprendre*, **30**: 97–105.

Schelling, T. (1974) *La tyrannie des petites décisions*, PUF, Paris.

Schelling, T. (1978) *Micro Motives, Macro Behaviours*, W.W. Norton.

Song, X.M., Montoya-Weiss, M.M. and Schmidt, J. (1997) 'Antecedents and consequences of cross-functional cooperation: a comparison of R&D, manufacturing and marketing perspectives', *Journal of Product Innovation Management*, **14**(1): 35–47.

Suleiman, E. (1979) *Les élites en France. Grand corps et grandes écoles*, Le Seuil, Paris.

Tannenbaum, R. *et al.* (1985) *Human Systems Development*, Jossey-Bass, San Francisco.

Taylor, F.W. (1913) *The Principles of Scientific Management*, Harper, New York.

Taylor, F.W. (1957) *La direction scientifique des entreprises*, Dunod, Paris.

Thievenard, J.-M. (1997) 'Insondable confiance.' In Laroche, M. *Le Monde Economie*, 28 January.

Thoenig, J. (1973) *L'ère des technocrates*, Editions d'Organisation, Paris.

Thureau-Dangin, P. (1995) *La concurrence et la mort*, Sifros, Paris.

Tichy, N. (1983) *Managing Strategic Change: Technical, Political and Cultural Dynamics*, John Wiley & Sons.

Tofler, A. (1990) *Powershift: Knowledge, Wealth and Violence at the Edge of the 21st Century*, Bantam Books, New York.

Tofler, A. (1991) *Les nouveaux pouvoirs*. Fayard, Paris.

Training (1993) 'Into the dark: rough ride ahead for American workers', July.

Uchitelle, L. (1997) 'The rehabilitation of Moning in America', *New York Times*, 23 February.

Ville, L. (1994) 'Grande Bretagne, le chômage diminue, l'emploi aussi', *Dossier de l'Expansion*, 478, 2–5 June.

Waterman, R.H. Jr (1995) *What America Does Right*, Penguin, New York.

Waterman, R.H. Jr, Peters, T.J. and Philips, J.R. (1980) 'Structure is not organization', *Business Horizons*, **23**(3): 14–26.

Weber, M. (1964) *Wirtschaft und Gesellschaft*, Berlin Kiepenhalter & Witsch, Cologne.

Weber, M. (1979) *Le savant et le politique*, Editions 10–18, Paris.

Weil, T. (1997) 'Provoquer les conflits: une pratique de bon management? A propos de deux articles de Kathleen M. Eisenhardt, Jeannie L. Eisenhardt et L.J. Bourgeois III', *Le Journal de l'Ecole de Paris*, **1**, January.

Williamson, O.E. (1975) *Markets and Hierarchies: Analysis and Antitrust Implications*, Free Press, New York.

Williamson, O.E. and Ouchi, W.G. (1981) 'The markets and hierarchies program of research: origins, implications, prospects'. In Van De Ven, A. and Joyce, W.F. (eds) *Perspectives on Design and Behaviour*, Wiley, New York, pp. 347–70.

Zarifian, P. (1993) *Quels nouveaux modèles d'organisation pour l'industrie européenne? L'émergence de la firm coopératrice*, L'Harmattan, Paris.